Marching To Slavery

South Africa's Descent Into Communism

by
Sipo E. Mzimela

Copyright © 1993
by
Rev. Sipo Mzimela

All rights reserved. No part of this book may be reproduced or transmitted in any form or by any means, electronic or mechanical, including photocopying, recording, or by any information storage and retrieval system, without permission in writing from the publishers. Published in the United States by Soundview Publications Inc.

For information regarding this book, write:
Soundview Publications Inc.
P.O. Box 467939, Atlanta, GA 30346-7939
or call:
1-800-728-2288

Dedication

To the young, innocent black South African boys and girls.

Whose remains are scattered in the jungles of Angola, Tanzania, Uganda, and Zambia. They were murdered by the African National Congress.

May They Rest in Peace.

And

To the Lost Generation, the millions of black South Africans whose futures were destroyed by the African National Congress.

May we never abandon them.

Acknowledgements

The list of people to whom I am indebted is far too long to be exhausted here. And there are people in South Africa who have helped, but their names I dare not publish. To do so would be to place their lives in mortal danger.

The original version of this manuscript was typed by Carole Whittington. Subsequent versions, including the final one, was typed by my eldest daughter Nomusa.

Sharon Dixon, who often had to meet unreasonable deadlines, read through all the drafts. Her criticisms, corrections, and suggestions were invaluable. I was greatly inspired by her ability and patience.

Thanks are due to Aida Parker for permission to use excerpts from: *What A Marxist South Africa Would Mean To You.*

Special mention must be made of my publishers at Soundview. For three years, Robert Kroening and Chip Wood worked patiently with me as changes in South Africa necessitated changes in the manuscript. Without their guidance, this book would not have been published. Dennis Wheeler edited the final manuscript. It was left to Joyce Morris to do the final proofreading.

My wife Gail, in addition to assisting with practical tasks, provided support and encouragement even when I doubted whether what became a time-consuming and frustrating task would ever be completed. Without her I probably would have given up.

I need only add that I am responsible for all the views expressed in this book.

Sipo E. Mzimela
Atlanta
Advent, 1993

Table of Contents

Chapter Title   Page

Introduction: Life in South Africa 1
Chapter One: Personal History 11
Chapater Two: The African National Congress:
    1912-1960 19
Chapter Three: Nelson Mandela 51
Chapter Four: Celebrity Churchmen 67
Chapter Five: The Anti-Apartheid Business
    International 77
Chapter Six: The Black American Mercenaries 93
Chapter Seven: The Curse of Modern Liberalism 109
Chapter Eight: The Inkatha Freedom Party 123
Chapter Nine: CODESA 143
Chapter Ten: The Lost Generation 163
Chapter Eleven: Which Road to Follow? 177
Chapter Twelve: The Road to Freedom 183
Chapter Thirteen: Freedom or Slavery? 189
Conclusion 197
Appendix I: How to Be a Good Communist 201
Appendix II: The Communist Inner Circle 221
Appendix III: A Memorial of War 225
Appendix IV: The Freedom Alliance 247
Index 251
Bibliography 259

Introduction

Life in South Africa

How can an outsider understand South Africa?

It is a country of stupendous, if sometimes enchanting, complexities. In a country where cultures from three continents — Africa, Asia, and Europe — meet, clash, coexist, and comingle, how could politics or daily life be simple? At the tip of the African continent, the Indian and Atlantic oceans come together with an unbridled energy that greatly influences South Africa's weather. In much the same way, these cultures converge to formulate the country's history, economy, religion, and politics.

The differences have played out over centuries in the peoples' languages, traditions, religions, and values. South Africa is the only country I know of where you could hear a person use four different South African languages in one sentence — and be understood by his listeners.

For over three centuries, black South Africans have had to survive oppression and attacks on their own varied cultures. They have developed a survival culture and a survival language for use with their oppressors. They understandably find the same tools useful when dealing with outsiders of any stripe. They can instinctively feed a questioner the answers they know the questioner wants to hear. Consequently, the news reported from South Africa by foreign journalists, or that packaged and sold by South African reporters, is not likely to be reliable or complete.

As a result, an outsider looking at the problems facing South Africa, just from the media point of view, would probably get about half of what is truly happening. So often the media portray the loud voice, for it is the easiest to hear. But, more times than not, the small voice that cannot be heard is the one that can make a positive contribution. Such is the case with South Africa.

Much of the confusion about South Africa is a result of centuries of propaganda which goes back to the time South Africa was colonized by the Dutch in 1652.

More Than a Country

To be sure, South Africa is not a country. It is one of Africa's five regions: North Africa, West Africa, East Africa, and Central Africa are the others. In each region there are several countries which are inhabited by different nations.

When European powers carved up Africa in the nineteenth century, they reshaped Africa by drawing artificial boundaries. In some cases, the result was people who belonged to the same nation were separated into two different countries, and in other cases, nations who had nothing in common were joined together in one country. The colonialists then expressed surprise that "black tribes" could and would not get along.

In South Africa, for example, the Swazi, Tswana, and Sotho were each split into separate countries by the arbitrary colonial lines. The Swazi in Swaziland are a nation; those in South Africa are said to be a tribe. It is the same with the Tswana and the Sotho. The other effect of colonialism in South Africa is that people who had nothing in common and are culturally very different from one another were locked into one geographic region but did not, however, become a nation. The boundaries were drawn after the black nations of the South African region — Sotho, Tswana, Xhosa, Qoi Qoi, Qoi San, Shangaan, Venda, Ndebele, Pedi, and Zulu were militarily defeated by the Afrikaner and the British. The indigenous peoples thus lost not only wars, but more important, their land

and their rights. It is important to emphasize that the black nations of South Africa were neither consulted nor did they give their consent when the Dutch and the English decided to make South Africa a country. This was a grave mistake which sowed the seeds of bitterness which in turn led to resistance, hatred, and now violence.

The task of building one united nation out of South Africa's diverse nations, cultures, races, languages, traditions, histories, customs, religions, ideologies, philosophies, expectations, stages of development, suspicions, hatreds, hopes, and fears, all of which are alive and vibrant, is a Herculean one, to say the least. It certainly cannot be accomplished overnight. Unfortunately the media often portray the conflict in South Africa as being essentially between blacks and whites. According to this view, all that needs to happen is that the white minority government be replaced by a black majority one. After that, so the argument goes, there will be peace and prosperity and everyone will live happily ever after. Hence the great international push for "one-person-one-vote" elections in April 1994. This kind of thinking is not only erroneous, but extremely dangerous.

My purpose in writing this book is to raise the level of the small voice so that it can be heard; it is an important voice. The title of the book points to the dangers facing post-apartheid South Africa, dangers which must be avoided at all cost.

If this book raises questions in the minds of some, answers questions for others, and encourages free, honest, and open discussion about South Africa, it will have served its purpose.

The Players

There are presently 26 political parties and organizations which are participating in negotiations that are intended to lead to a formal end of apartheid and the birth of a new, democratic South Africa. There are several other parties which the government and the ANC have excluded from the negotiations. This undemocratic act raises grave questions, especially about the intentions of the National Party government and the ANC. Not all parties and organizations are of equal strength. Some have more support than others. Since there has never been a nonracial, all-inclusive election, no one knows the real strength of each political organization. It is generally assumed that the following players will have to find a common ground if civil war is to be avoided.

The African National Congress (ANC): The ANC was formed in 1912 by black Christians. The original name was the South African Native National Congress. This was changed to African National Congress (ANC) in 1923.

The ANC was formed in order to address two important issues. The first was the question of citizenship for black South Africans. In 1910, white South Africans, with the blessing of the British government, formed the Union of South Africa and excluded blacks from citizenship. The second reason was to unite all the black nations within the geographic region of Southern Africa, and, through this win important concessions from the white government. This would be achieved by using Gandhi's principles of nonviolent resistance. Thus the organization was originally Christian, reformist, and nonviolent. In 1921, the Communist Party of South Africa (CPSA) was formed by white South Africans who sought to influence the ANC. At the time, this move was successfully resisted.

Even though the ANC remained a nonviolent movement, it was banned in 1960 by the South African government. Some of the ANC leaders went underground and others into exile. The banning weakened the ANC and strengthened the hand of the communists. In 1961 the communists, who had changed their name to the South African Communist Party, formed a military wing and called it *Umkhonto WeSizwe* (MK). It became known as the military wing of the ANC. The original pillars of the ANC — Christian, reformist, and nonviolent — were removed. The organization became a violent revolutionary movement.

In 1985 the SACP merged with the ANC. This move effectively transformed the ANC into a front for the Communist Party. The ANC claims to have a registered membership of 400,000. Yet, almost all of its funding is from overseas. Sweden alone gives the ANC over $10 million a year.

The ANC also has a youth league (ANCYL). It too, has been very active in perpetrating murder and mayhem throughout South Africa. The Youth League's slogan is direct: "Kill a Boer, kill a farmer."

The Conservative Party (CP): The Conservative Party was formed in 1982 by members of the white parliament who broke away from the governing National Party (NP) over the issue of reforming apartheid. The CP objected to the government's announced policy of giving political rights to blacks in a unified South Africa.

Support for the CP, which was originally limited to Afrikaans-speaking white South Africans, has grown to include other white South Africans such as the English and Portuguese. In South Africa it is widely believed that the CP has the support of the South African military establishment.

Inkatha Freedom Party (IFP): What is known today as Inkatha Freedom Party (IFP) has a long history. The original organization was *Inkatha YakwaZulu* which was a Zulu cultural organization, formed in 1928 by the Zulu King Solomon ka Dinizulu. The organization lasted only a few years.

In 1975, Dr. Mangosuthu Buthelezi resurrected the name Inkatha and formed *Inkatha Yenkululeko Yesizwe*. Membership was opened to all black South Africans.

The formation of the organization in 1975 marked the rebirth of the original ANC which was Christian, reformist, and nonviolent. Inkatha opposed both the sanctions campaign against South Africa and the ANC's armed struggle. This led first to tension between the two organizations and finally to the current low-level civil war. In 1990, Inkatha transformed itself from a liberation movement to a political party.

There are approximately 2.5 million registered members in the party. These include large numbers of white South Africans who see the IFP as the only hope for South Africa.

The National Party (NP): In 1914, two years after the formation of the ANC, a group of Afrikaners formed an exclusive Afrikaner party — the National Party. The aim was not only to separate black, white, colored, and Indian South Africans, but also to make the Afrikaners the sole rulers of South Africa.

Afrikaner intellectuals and theologians justified their policy of apartheid (separateness) with selective quotations from scripture and theological formulations. They argued that since God created different races, he does not want them to mix. Some even stated that the Afrikaner nation was the new Israel and South Africa the new Canaan, given to them by God. Apartheid rested on the twin pillars of racial purity and racial superiority.

After winning the general election in 1948, the NP passed the interlocking laws which defined the apartheid state. Between 1948 and 1990, thousands of apartheid laws, regulations, and decrees were put into place. In order to prevent any black uprising, the NP government spent billions of dollars on security measures which included such institutions as the military and police as well as a network of informers and hit squads.

For more than forty years, the NP defied calls from the rest of the world to abandon apartheid and unify the country. These fell on deaf ears. In 1990, the National Party "changed course," announcing that it would abandon apartheid and introduce democracy into South Africa.

Because of its new policies, over the past two years, the National Party has lost much of its support. So much so that if another "all-white" election were to be held, the NP would probably not win a majority. There can be no doubt that the days of National Party glory are over.

The Pan Africanist Congress (PAC): The Pan Africanist Congress was formed in 1959 by a group that broke away from the ANC. The group objected to the cooperation between the ANC and white liberals, irrationally arguing that whites had no interest in the liberation of blacks. The group also objected to the presence of communists within the ANC. The PAC was therefore formed as a black nationalist movement and attracted many black intellectuals. Its slogan was "Africa for the Africans."

The PAC became very popular and by the end of 1959 had more registered members than the ANC. It is the PAC which organized the march against passes in 1960 in Sharpesville. Police opened fire on the demonstrators, killing many of them.

The government reacted to the growing strength of the PAC by banning both the PAC and the ANC. Both organizations established themselves in exile. Once out of the country, the PAC established its own military wing, the Azania People's Liberation Army (APLA). Members of APLA have claimed responsibility for the recent, high-profile killing of whites. This includes the murderous attack on a church in a Cape Town suburb in which 10 churchgoers were killed as they worshipped.

PAC refers to South Africa as Azania. Their new slogan has become: "One settler, one bullet." This means that every white in South Africa is to be shot. This slogan has been chanted by large crowds in stadium rallies, and was the cry when the American student, Amy Biehl, was murdered in a township outside of Cape Town.

While the popular media in South Africa erroneously refer to the ANC as the largest black political organization, most of the blacks who support revolution in South Africa identify with the PAC rather than the ANC. This reality led to the formation of the "Patriotic Front" in 1991; an alliance between the ANC and the PAC. *Economist* (November 2, 1991) reported: "Real politics put down fresh roots when on October 27th, South Africa's two main 'liberation movements' got together to form the Patriotic Front.... Cynics suspected that the formation of the Patriotic Front would mask a takeover by the ANC of the smaller PAC, which split off in 1959."

Because of this alliance, we know that violent acts committed by the PAC have the backing of the ANC, and vice versa.

The South African Communist Party (SACP): In 1921, the Communist Party of South Africa (CPSA) was formed and affiliated with the Moscow Comintern. At that time communists in South Africa took their instructions from Moscow. The name was changed to the South African Communist Party in 1953.

That racism played a part in the formation is clear not just from the fact that it was an all-white party, but also from the party's slogan which was "Workers of the world unite and fight for a white South Africa."

In 1924, the CPSA was instructed from Moscow to admit black members. This policy was based on the conclusion that before South Africa could become a communist state, a black government would have to be in power.

The CPSA was the first political party to be banned by the South African government in 1950. However, the members went underground and renamed the party the South African Communist Party (SACP) in 1953. The Freedom Charter, which is often referred to as an ANC document, was drawn up by the SACP in 1955. The SACP is also indirectly responsible for the formation of the PAC. In 1961, the SACP formed an armed wing of the ANC, and called it Umkhonto WeSizwe. In 1985 the SACP effectively took over the leadership of the ANC.

Although the party has only 3,500 members, it wields enormous influence, especially among the black urban youth.

The SACP, which is a neo-Stalinist party supportive of both Fidel Castro and Saddam Hussein, still maintains that communism is not just the best solution for South Africa, but is an achievable goal. The party's control of the ANC, the urban black youth, and the largest black trade union, COSATU, should not be dismissed as a passing phase.

The Volksfront: The Volksfront was formed in 1993 and has under its umbrella a wide range of white, anti-communist organizations. The "Front" is opposed to what has emerged as an alliance of the ANC, the NP, and the South African Communist Party and demands a separate homeland for the Afrikaners. It is led by ex-military personnel and, together with the Conservative Party, commands the allegiance of most of the security forces.

In addition to these seven parties and organizations there are more than 20 other political parties. At least 19 of them are involved in the multi-party talks which started in December 1990.

The large number of political parties and organizations which represent a variety of political and economic ideologies should result in lively and interesting debates and discussions leading to broad-based agreements. Such would be the case in a country with a democratic tradition.

South Africa, though, has no democratic foundation to build on and no experience of negotiations. For more than 300 years, the country has known only dictatorship. Only time will tell whether an acceptable solution will be achieved through negotiations or whether a solution will be forced through a civil war.

Chapter 1

Personal History

I was born before the advent of apartheid in South Africa. The neighborhood where my family lived reflected the racial mix of South Africa. There were blacks who spoke a variety of African languages, especially Zulu, Xhosa, and Sotho. There were Indians who spoke Hindi and Tamil. Coloreds spoke English or Afrikaans or Zulu and the white children spoke either English or Afrikaans.

Thus, we grew up speaking several languages. As children, we played together and spoke a language peculiar to South Africa. It is called Fanakalo, which is a concoction of several languages and has a strong Zulu base. We also learned at a very early age to use several languages in one sentence. The boys played soccer or football as we called it, and the girls played basketball. Boys and girls together played "round us," which was a modified version of baseball.

During my formative years, racial differences had no meaning for me. In fact, my best friend was Tommy, a white boy whose parents had a dairy farm where we bought our milk. We went to the same local church and talked about being priests when we grew up. We also both loved dogs. His family had five and we had two.

Neither my mother nor father had much of a formal education. My mother had six years of formal education and my father had four. They were both hard-working and although poor, wanted the best for us. From a very early age we were taught discipline, honesty, and respect. We were taught that education is the key to the future. We had to work hard. We were taught to have faith in prayer. We found that the extended family provided a great deal of support and warmth. What I was taught at home was reinforced by my teachers at school and the Christian community at church.

My parents were members of the Anglican Church and the African National Congress. My three sisters and I, as well as our cousins, nephews, and nieces, learned at a very early age that the ANC wanted everyone to respect one another and all South Africans to be treated fairly — something we children already experienced on the playing fields. It is fair to say that my parents sowed in us the seeds of Christianity and the ANC ideals at the same time when we were of tender age.

Life Under Apartheid

In 1950, when I was 15 years old, I experienced the horror of apartheid for the first time. The area where I lived was declared a "white" area by the government. It meant that all the families that were not white had to move. Worse still, all those blacks who were not born in the cities where they lived had to return to their tribal homelands. That meant the breaking up of our extended family. Some of the members were forced to return to the rural areas.

One day at the break of dawn, police trucks arrived and we were given an hour to load our belongings. We would be moved to an unknown location. An hour later, what had been home was reduced to rubble by government bulldozers. I cried. I think everybody cried. I can still hear the dogs barking as if they were in agony. I will never forget my grandfather's words as he stood gazing at what had been home. He said, "We blacks have a duty to show and teach whites what it means to be human." As we were driven away, I thought of Tommy. I would not see him that day after school. In fact, I never saw him again. I have often wondered what happened to him.

The reign of terror which was unleashed against blacks by the South African government forced the ANC to call on black South Africans to participate in a nonviolent defiance campaign. All unjust laws were to be defied. ANC members and supporters were urged, for example, not to carry passes especially in the evenings when blacks in the cities were subject to curfew laws. They were also encouraged to use facilities reserved for whites only.

In 1952, when I was in high school, I formally joined the ANC after listening to the president of the movement. Chief Albert Lutuli had urged us at a rally in the city of Durban, to "launch out into the deep." I was arrested twice for deliberately breaking the curfew. For me, participation in the nonviolent defiance campaign was part of my Christian duty to fight evil and struggle for justice. I know from my reading of the scriptures that those who challenge the evil powers of this world must often pay the price by being imprisoned or killed.

The more we engaged in peaceful opposition to apartheid, the more brutal the South African government became. In the process we became more politicized as we struggled with the emotional pain caused by seeing fellow white Christians beat us up, arrest, torture, and kill us for no reason except that we had a dark skin color. In spite of all this, I had not lost my faith either in what the ANC stood for — a just and democratic South Africa — or in the power of the gospel to eventually destroy evil.

The Birth of the ANC Military

In 1960, however, the shooting of peaceful demonstrators in Sharpeville and other realities of apartheid forced me to leave the church I wanted to serve as a priest. The ANC and PAC were banned at the same time.

The following year, we learned from what we thought were ANC underground sources, that Mandela and others had formed a "military wing of the ANC" in Johannesburg. This military wing was called Umkhonto WeSizwe (MK), which means Spear of the Nation. They argued that since the government would not negotiate with blacks, the only available response to the government's use of force was guerrilla warfare. The argument was so persuasive that many of us went underground and left the country. We would train as guerrillas, just as Mandela had done, and return to topple the oppressive white government. Once in Tanzania, we discovered that not all of us could become guerrillas. Only those who had not finished high school were sent for military training. The rest of us were sent for further education.

We also discovered — much to our surprise — that MK had actually been founded by the illegal South African Communist Party, which also operated from underground with headquarters in Johannesburg. Mandela had been chosen by the Communist Party as the first Commander of MK.

In the communist camps in Tanzania, Chinese instructors introduced us to the theory of guerrilla warfare, how to organize the loyal communities, how to prepare and use propaganda, and how to set up a security network.

Western countries refused to give scholarships, travel documents, or any other kind of assistance to those of us chosen for education. An American diplomat in Dar-es-Salem, capital of Tanzania, told me that only those who had escaped from communist countries would receive help from the U.S. South Africans, he said, did not qualify. East European countries, on the other hand, accepted us without preconditions. This convinced us that our only friends in the struggle for freedom were the communists.

Life in the Communist Underground

My scholarship took me to Czechoslovakia, where I had the unforgettable experience of studying Marxist theory in the classroom while living in a communist state and interacting with Czechs. The contradiction between theory and practice could not have been clearer.

In the town of Dobruska (pronounced Do-broosh-ka), where our school was located, we tasted life under communism. The Czechs believed that all Third World students would return to their countries of origin after finishing their studies and become communist leaders. Therefore, they tried to show us what life was like for communist leaders. I remember being invited to the home of the mayor of Dobruska for dinner. He had a beautiful house, well-furnished and spacious. To my utter surprise, he served refreshment I had thought unavailable in Czechoslovakia, including orange juice, ginger ale, and American soft drinks. I thought the Czechs drank only beer — which was exceptionally good — and vodka. But he had Russian Krim Champagne and an assortment of other expensive international alcoholic beverages. The meal, too, was outstanding. The talk centered around the evils of capitalism and its impending demise. He was convinced that we were destined to become the leaders of a great, new, socialist Africa. I believed him. After all, Marxist theory, political economy, and the history of imperialism and capitalism which we digested in the classroom, confirmed what the mayor was saying.

Unfortunately for the mayor and our teachers, we spent a great deal of time with Czech workers. From them we learned the truth about communism. In one of the local pubs which we frequented in the evenings, we talked with people who were highly educated, but had been demoted and forced to work as laborers because they had been part of the capitalist system. It was not unusual to hear a Czech saying in perfect English: "I am a former physics professor. I was demoted by the communist regime." The Czech workers hated communism. They longed for the "old days" before they became a Soviet satellite state.

I visited several Czech homes. Conditions were appalling. People virtually lived on potatoes and cabbage and very fat pork. They lived in cramped apartments. Even worse, they lived in total fear of being arrested and sent to Siberia. They did not discuss the politics of their country or any East European country. They knew very little about the outside world except that the West was capitalist and an enemy of the rest of the world. I was shocked at their ignorance.

Perhaps the most shocking discovery for me was the existence of racism in a socialist country. Many Czechs resented foreign students because they felt their government was spending their money educating foreigners and Czechs had to make too many sacrifices. To make matters worse, African diplomats drove Mercedes Benzes, which no Czech could afford and foreign students wore western clothes, including jeans, which were superior in quality and unavailable to Czechs. Resentment often led to fist fights. Some of the fights were tragic. For example, in February 1964, a student from Mali was thrown into the icy Voltava River in Prague because he had a Czech girlfriend. A Zambian student was thrown off a moving train for the same reason. He broke his spine. Both Mali and Zambia withdrew all their students from Czechoslovakia.

In the end, I decided that communism was not only a fraud, it was worse than apartheid.

Moving to the West

Disillusioned, I left for West Germany, where I experienced for the first time what it was like to live in a democracy. West Germany gave me an education, material rewards, and new hope for South Africa. If the Germans could emerge from the darkest depths of racial tyranny and build a solid, free, and democratic society, surely we could do the same.

In 1974, after spending a decade in West Germany, I left for the United States where I would enter seminary and study for holy orders in the Episcopal Church. The successful completion of training and the ordination which followed marked the fulfillment of my aborted childhood dream.

I lived in New York from 1974 to 1980 and worked with the ANC's Observer Mission to the United Nations and United States. I gained invaluable experience at the UN as the

ANC's deputy representative. I also worked closely with many anti-apartheid groups across the U.S., and in Canada and Europe.

I was among those exiled members of the ANC who firmly believed in a political end to apartheid. I felt the international community would support our cause if we remained faithful to the ideals of the founding fathers of the ANC.

I considered Umkhonto WeSizwe mere propaganda at best and saw no way they could overthrow the South African government militarily. Disagreement abounded among exiles as to the strategy we should follow. I maintained that the function of the exiles was to articulate to the outside world what victims of apartheid inside South Africa were feeling, saying, and doing. I believed the ANC-in-exile had no right to make decisions without consulting the membership inside South Africa. Unfortunately, only a few of us thought this way. Many in the leadership acted as though the ANC were a government-in-exile, with headquarters in Lusaka, Zambia and an embassy in New York. The ANC actually did have a real embassy in communist East Berlin.

In June 1985, exiled leaders of the ANC merged the organization with the South African Communist Party. The formation of the ANC/South African Communist Party Alliance was the death-blow to what had once been a great and respectable movement. Those of us who rejected communism and illicit violence as means to political power were abandoned. The real ANC died in 1985. Only the name remained. The movement became a front for the South African Communist Party. I resigned from the movement that had been part of me for 32 years.

Chapter 2

The African National Congress: 1912-1960

What the ANC Stood For

On January 8, 1912, a group of African leaders, traditional chiefs, educators, lawyers, and pastors met in the city of Bloemfontein, in the Province of the Orange Free State. This is an Afrikaner stronghold. They founded the South African Native National Congress (SANNC). Delegates came not just from South Africa, but also from what is now Lesotho, Botswana, and Zambia. They had one thing in common: They were all victims of colonialism and they wanted to be free.

The history of how Africa was colonized and divided among European powers in the 19th century is written in blood. Nowhere on the continent of Africa was more blood shed than in South Africa, and no nation fought more wars, or lost more people than the Zulus.

The Zulus inflicted the greatest defeat in African history on the British. Armed only with spears and shields, the Zulus annihilated a well-trained British force which was armed to the teeth with fire power. At the battle of Isandlwana in 1879, the British lost more men in one day than they have ever lost in any battle, including the second World War. That battle marked the greatest humiliation the British have ever suffered.

In 1906, however, the Zulus were finally crushed by the British. The Zulus are not ashamed. They respected their conquerors and conceded the futility of trying to confront guns with spears.

After 1906, Zulu leaders decided that to restore Zulu dignity and the dignity of all black South Africans who had been robbed of their land and rights by the colonizers, they must negotiate. The driving force behind the call for a black organization that would negotiate with the British government was the Zulus. The Zulus, therefore, were largely responsible for the formation of the original South African National Native Congress, later the African National Congress, in 1912.

The founding fathers of the SANNC were devout Christian men. At their opening session they sang *Lizalis'indinga Lakho Thixo Nkose Yenyaniso* (Fulfill Thy Promise, God, Thou Lord of Truth). The first elected President was the Rev. Dr. John L. Dube, an American-educated Methodist minister, who was so inspired by Booker T. Washington, that on his return to South Africa, he founded Ohlange Institute, the only educational institution ever established by a black in South Africa, and my alma mater.

The SANNC was founded for two reasons. The first was to end tribalism. Dr. Pixley Ka Isaka Seme, a graduate of Columbia University in New York and the convener of the conference wrote: "The demon of racialism, the aberrations of the Xhosa-Fingo feud, the animosity that exists between the Zulus and the Tsongas, between the Basutho and every other native, must be buried and forgotten. These divisions, these jealousies, are the cause of our woes and all the backwardness and ignorance that exists today." Seme is the founding father of the original Christian ANC.

The second reason was to seek concessions from the British and South African governments so that blacks could be represented equitably in the all-white Parliament and discrimination gradually lifted, particularly against the "educated natives." Thus, the founding fathers of the SANNC were Christian, reformist, and pragmatic.

Little headway was made, either in uniting blacks or in getting white South Africans to accommodate black participation. The Land Acts of 1913 and 1936 effectively gave

87 percent of the land to white South Africans and reserved only 13 percent for blacks. The ANC made many overtures to the government in South Africa and the British government in London. In England, ANC delegations were treated politely, but went back to South Africa empty-handed. At the signing of the Peace of Versailles after World War I, an ANC delegation was present to press for concessions. Again, nothing was forthcoming.

When all appeals failed, the SANNC organized peaceful demonstrations against injustice, especially the hated pass laws. The South African government refused to listen to the moderate black voice of reason. In 1919 an anti-pass demonstration was organized. This action resulted in the arrest of some 700 people. In 1920, forty thousand miners went on strike and 21 people were killed by police. By contrast, over 100 Qoi San people were killed in 1924 for refusing to pay a dog tax!

On July 30, 1921, the Communist Party of South Africa (CPSA) was formed as an all-white party. Its slogan was "Workers of the World unite and save a White South Africa!" The name of SANNC was changed to ANC (African National Congress) in 1923. When, however, the South African government announced its intention in 1924 to make South Africa "a white man's country" the CPSA, in an effort to distance itself from the government, changed its language and said: "Our main revolutionary task is among the natives." Some blacks in Johannesburg did join the CPSA. Others showed willingness to cooperate with the CPSA. One such black was Josiah Gumede, who during his tenure as president of the ANC, even visited the Soviet Union. By that time, the CPSA had announced that its policy would be "the extension of the Party's influence wherever possible in native bodies like the African National Congress" (*The Amazing Mr. Fischer*; G. Ludi and B. Grobbelar, Nasionale Boekhandel, Cape Town, 1966,

p. 8). Gumede's decision to cooperate with communists alarmed the rank and file ANC membership. He was voted out of office after serving only three years as president.

A number of black cultural organizations were formed during this period. One of them was Inkatha, which was formed in 1928 as a Zulu organization, with the purpose of preserving Zulu culture at a time when industrialization was threatening it. The movement, however, did not survive very long. The original Inkatha movement was a purely cultural/social organization and had nothing to do with politics.

In 1943, the ANC Youth League (ANCYL) was formed. Its members included Oliver Tambo, Nelson Mandela, and Walter Sisulu. The ANCYL had within its ranks Marxists like Tambo, Mandela, and Sisulu and also fierce opponents of Marxism, men who believed in Africanism and were Christians. The latter included Anton Lembede, a Roman Catholic and first president of the ANCYL. Africanism meant pride in the culture and history of Africans, determination to overcome oppression, and a belief that the entire African continent had a common destiny. This last idea was not new. In 1897, Enoch Sontonga, a teacher and Methodist had written the first verse of a hymn entitled *"Nkosi Sikelel'iAfrika"* (God Bless Africa, including all of Africa, not just the southern tip of the continent). Lembede was succeeded by another anti-communist as president of ANCYL. He was Peter Mda, who, because of ill-health, did not serve very long.

During this period, the ANC was led by Dr. Alfred Xuma, who, among other things, gave equality to women within the ANC in 1940! A devout Christian, he was tireless in his efforts to build the ANC as a pragmatic, reformist organization.

At the 1949 annual conference of the ANC, the Marxist wing of the ANCYL staged a coup by ousting Dr. Xuma and replacing him with Dr. Moroka, a man who because he was extremely weak and had no leadership qualities, they rightly believed could be easily manipulated and controlled. Walter

Sisulu was elected secretary general, and two other black communists, Dan Tloome and Moses Kotane, a graduate of the Lenin School in Moscow, were also elected to the ANC's National Executive Committee (NEC). In 1990, on the day of his release from prison, Nelson Mandela saluted the communist Moses Kotane as a champion for democracy! The 1949 conference also adopted a "Programme of Action" which called for strikes, boycotts, resistance, and general civil disobedience, but not violence.

The white National Party government, came to power in 1948 and instituted apartheid. In 1950 it introduced the Unlawful Organizations Bill, which was intended to ban the CPSA. The CPSA disbanded and went underground, where it reconstituted itself as the South African Communist Party (SACP). Many black members of the disbanded CPSA joined the ANC, bringing with them considerable communist influence. All of this took place in Johannesburg and led to turmoil within the ranks of the ANC. The communists were bent on taking over.

In fact, not all members of the ANC were happy with admitting communists into the movement. Some devout Christians believed communism was diametrically opposed to Christianity. They left the ANC because of this. One prominent member who left was Bishop Alphaeus Zulu, the first black Anglican bishop of South Africa. The majority, however, thought that since the ANC was a movement which welcomed all those who were opposed to oppression and discrimination, communists could not be barred from membership unless they tried to turn the movement into a communist front. Up to this moment, however, the communists had failed in their grand design of taking over the ANC.

The annual conference of the ANC in December 1952 was the most chaotic in the movement's history. Chief Albert Lutuli, who did not seek office, was elected ANC president. He turned out to be the last elected president of the ANC and its greatest. This Christian lay preacher and great Zulu chief restored order to the movement, returning it to its ethos: Christian, reformist, pragmatic, non-violent. With Lutuli at the helm of the ANC, the campaign of disciplined, non-violent civil disobedience, which became known as the Defiance Campaign, spread throughout the country like wildfire. The strategy was based on the philosophy and actions of Mahatma Gandhi who had started passive resistance in South Africa before returning to India to lead his own people. Lutuli turned the ANC into a well-organized movement. During his tenure as president, whites, coloreds, and Asians participated with the ANC in defying unjust laws. Lutuli earned international respect for the ANC. This lasted until 1969 when ANC opponents began to link the name of the ANC with brutal acts of terror against fellow blacks in South Africa.

Cooperation among whites, coloreds, blacks, and Asians under Lutuli resulted in the convening of what was dubbed the "Congress of the People." Over 2,800 delegates representing the ANC, the South African Indian Congress, the South African Colored Peoples' Organization, and the Congress of Democrats (a white communist organization) met in Kliptown, outside Johannesburg, in June of 1955. They came to discuss the future of South Africa. It was this group, representing blacks, whites, Indians, and coloreds, which adopted the Freedom Charter. The Freedom Charter is not an ANC document as is often claimed. It was largely the work of the white communist Congress of Democrats. Its Marxist language is clear: "... the mineral wealth beneath the soil, the banks and the monopoly industries shall be transferred to the people as a whole" (Freedom Charter).

Apart from the preamble which states that South Africa belongs to all her people, the Freedom Charter is irrelevant in this day and age. It was drawn up at a time when people in many parts of the world looked to communism as the world's future economic, political, and social order. Events throughout the world have since proved that prediction wrong. Yet,

Mandela, who was obviously oblivious to this fact, used the obsolete Freedom Charter's language in 1990 when he said an "ANC" government would nationalize the mines, banks, and monopoly industries.

ANC President Albert Lutuli, a man of great courage, vision, and integrity had consistently rejected calls from the communist wing of the ANC to radicalize the movement. He made it clear that the ANC was a movement for democracy, not a political party. The ANC never intended to form a government and rule South Africa. Its objective was to have blacks included in all areas of decision-making. The ANC campaigned for blacks, coloreds, Indians, and whites to participate fully and equally in governing South Africa. His message gained him a large following even among whites, including some conservatives.

After the 1955 adoption of the Freedom Charter by the Congress of the People, the South African government panicked and arrested its leaders. In all, 156 people were arrested and charged with high treason. The trial lasted from 1956 to 1961. The prosecution never proved its case and all the defendants were acquitted.

Meanwhile, the growth of the communist influence within the ranks of the ANC led to a split in the movement in 1958 and the formation of the anti-communist Pan Africanist Congress (PAC) in early 1959. The PAC declared that it was the "custodian of ANC policy as formulated in 1912" (*Black Politics in South Africa Since 1912*: p. 7). The PAC also adopted the slogan "Africa for the Africans" and initially limited its membership to blacks only. Many people accused it of being a racist organization. In March 1960, the PAC organized a demonstration against the hated pass laws in Sharpeville near Johannesburg. The peaceful demonstration was brutally crushed by police. Sixty-nine black men, women, and children were shot dead and over two 200 injured.

The white government reacted by banning both the ANC and PAC and declared a state of emergency. With the bannings came the arrest, detention, and banishment of the top leadership of both organizations. Chief Albert Lutuli was banished to his farm and muzzled. The president of the PAC, Robert Sobukwe and one of his top lieutenants, were jailed on Robben Island, the maximum security prison later made famous by Nelson Mandela. Before the bannings, the ANC had sent Oliver Tambo overseas as a roving ambassador to mobilize international support for freedom in South Africa. This was part of the ANC's non-violent campaign which was rooted in the faith that good triumphs over evil if people of good will work hard through non-violent means.

It is important to emphasize that the apartheid government did not ban the ANC in 1960 because the organization had become violent. The ANC was banned primarily because under the leadership of Chief Albert Lutuli, an increasing number of white South Africans were becoming convinced that apartheid was immoral and had no future. This alarmed the government which, like all dictators, took measures to silence the voice of reason and truth.

The banning of the ANC and PAC in 1960, as well as the arrest, imprisonment, detentions, and banishment of the leadership of the two organizations, dealt a heavy blow to the nonviolent struggle of black South Africans. It also paved the way for opportunists and criminals to take over the organizations once they were being operated in exile.

The violence which now plagues South Africa is a direct consequence of the National Party's draconian steps of banning peaceful black organizations in 1960.

Another consequence of the banning was the successful takeover of the ANC by the South African Communist Party. We must now turn to the question of how a Christian, nonviolent ANC became a murderous communist front.

What the ANC Has Become

As stated earlier, the original African National Congress was formed to unite all black South Africans. As such, the original ANC was unapologetically a black movement for black people, born out of the unique experience and the reality in which black people in South Africa found themselves. The original ANC, therefore, was not a political party. It was not even known as a liberation movement. It was a congress which brought together diverse groups of black people. There was no ideology, only a quest for freedom and participation.

In 1961, the banned, underground communist movement founded *Umkhonto WeSizwe* (Spear of the Nation), normally referred to as MK. In order to mislead people, MK was called "military wing of the ANC." In reality, MK had nothing to do with the ANC. The ANC never officially decided to form a "military wing." The very idea went against everything that the ANC stood for: Christianity, reform, pragmatism, and above all, non-violence. Black South Africans have a long history of warfare against whites. If, in 1960, they had decided once again to resort to violence, they would have joined MK by the thousands. This did not happen. The formation of MK marked only the triumph of a process designed to destroy the non-violent ANC and replace it with a violent, Marxist revolutionary movement. The process had started in 1943 with the formation of the communist-inspired African National Congress Youth League. The younger members, including Nelson Mandela, accused the ANC leadership of being enslaved to a "dying order of pseudo-liberalism and conservatism, of appeasement and compromise."

If MK had not been formed, the original ANC would have legally reappeared under a different name. There was precedence for this. After all, South Africa was not the first country to ban black political movements. In Rhodesia — now Zimbabwe — when the government banned the African National Congress in 1958, the movement re-emerged as the National Democratic Party. When that was banned in 1960, the same movement reappeared as the Zimbabwe African People's Union with the national executive, ethos, and membership unchanged.

When MK was launched, the South African Communist Party could not afford to be seen as the founders of the movement. In order to gain support, they reasoned, MK had to have a black face even though power would remain in white and Indian hands.

Significantly, the man the white communists chose as the first Commander of MK — its black face — was Nelson Mandela, a man who had never held elected office in the ANC. Mandela had no legitimate authority to change the ethos and program of the ANC. The whites and Indians knew that Mandela was ambitious, power-hungry, reckless, and opportunistic; therefore perfect for the job. ANC President Albert Lutuli was never consulted. Since he was muzzled and banished to his farm in Natal, the SACP in Johannesburg, some 700 miles away, was free to speak and act as it pleased. The South African government, by banning a non-violent ANC, gave license to the communists to introduce a reign of terror under the guise of MK and the famous armed struggle. This reign of terror, which started in 1961, now threatens to plunge the country into a full-scale, catastrophic civil war with the communists and their left-leaning liberal allies on the one side and those who want real freedom on the other.

Even under the humiliation of banning and muzzling, Lutuli remained committed to non-violence and a truly democratic, non-racial South Africa. This total commitment to non-violent change won Lutuli the Nobel Peace Price which he received in 1961. Lutuli became the first African ever to win the Prize. This recognition alarmed the SACP. They feared that the government would recognize the wisdom of dealing with a non-violent, pragmatic movement and unban the ANC.

In order to destroy any such chance, it was announced from underground in 1961 that MK was "the military wing of the ANC." The message was intended to send a clear signal to the government that the ANC had abandoned non-violence and reform, opting instead for violence to achieve political goals. Nothing could have been farther from the truth.

A few days after Lutuli received the Peace Prize, MK committed its first acts of terror by exploding several bombs in the Transvaal. As mentioned previously, by the time the ANC was banned in 1960, Lutuli had built up a substantial following among white South Africans, coloreds, and Indians. The MK bombings were timed to end this support.

In August of 1962, Nelson Mandela was arrested while on one of his foolish underground missions of violence. The American media have suggested, ignorantly, that Mandela's capture was the work of the CIA. Rather, the vast majority of blacks who still considered themselves ANC deeply resented the way their beloved organization was linked with senseless acts of terror. A member of the banned ANC reported Mandela's whereabouts to the police. The informant was one of many who wanted an end to terror and viewed Mandela as an impostor because he was never elected by the people to be their leader. He was, and to this day remains, a shackled slave of his masters — white and Indian communists. Mandela was accused of inciting people to strike illegally and leaving the country without a valid passport. He was convicted on November 7, 1962, and sentenced to five years in prison.

In July 1963, ten members of the "High Command" of MK were arrested in Rivonia near Johannesburg. Captured documents revealed the membership of MK and Mandela was listed as a member of the High Command. If Lutuli or any other non-communist legitimate officials of the African National Congress had anything to do with Umkhonto WeSizwe, their names would have been listed in the captured documents. If MK were truly the "military wing of the ANC," then the ANC President, Chief Albert Lutuli, would have been the Commander-in-Chief. He had nothing to do with MK. The great lie that linked MK to the ANC had been fabricated by the South African Communist Party and supported by the western liberal media.

Out of the ten accused, eight were found guilty and sentenced to life imprisonment. To be fair, in any other

African country, had they been lucky enough to have trials, they would have been sentenced to death. In Nigeria, Ghana, Liberia, Sudan, Ethiopia, Chad, Uganda, Burundi, and Somalia those who had tried to overthrow unpopular governments were executed by firing squad without the benefit of a trial. Those same countries are among the harshest critics of the white South African government.

With the SACP/MK underground network within South Africa destroyed, and with no hope that the ban on the ANC and PAC would ever be lifted, the struggle for liberation of South Africa shifted to the international arena.

A number of ANC regional leaders left South Africa secretly and soon the number of exiles swelled. Lutuli objected to this exodus, fearing that it would leave blacks within the country without effective leadership. Almost all of the exiles became involved in educating the outside world about the horrors of apartheid. Chief Lutuli died in 1967 and Oliver Tambo, who was already in exile, became the de facto leader of the ANC-in-exile. Tambo was never elected leader of the ANC. In a properly constituted annual conference of the original ANC, Tambo would not have been considered for the post of president. Dull, weak, uninspiring, sheepish, and corrupt, Tambo fell easy prey to cunning and well-organized communists.

In 1969 in Morogoro, Tanzania, an unrepresentative conference of the ANC convened and was manipulated into transforming the organization into a multiracial one. Thus Joseph Slovo, a white man, soon to become chairman of the South African Communist Party, joined the ANC. Many white communists openly joined the ANC. Joseph Slovo also became commander-in-chief of MK, an astounding development.

The agenda of the original ANC, changing South Africa through peaceful means, had not been abandoned with the banning of the movement in 1960. Dedicated men and women, while still in exile, believed that if the international community would take specific non-violent actions against apartheid, the South African government would capitulate.

In exile, the ANC clearly included two distinct groups: a non-violent group and a group that believed in violence. The non-violent group was made up of non-communists. The communists belonged to the violent group. In exile, "ANC" stood for both African National Congress and African National Communists. The acronym "ANC" is therefore confusing.

The task of enlisting international support for the fight against apartheid was left to the non-violent group. The members of this group appealed to the so-called "international community" to isolate the apartheid regime through sport and cultural boycotts, disinvestment, sanctions, withdrawal of diplomatic recognition, and travel restrictions.

Indeed, this group was in reality the original ANC within the new communist-led ANC. It can rightly claim credit for establishing a supportive international network known as the Anti-Apartheid Movement (AAM), whose success has no parallel in history. Governments, trade unions, the media, religious organizations, educational institutions, political parties, prestigious international organizations, and individuals across the globe rallied around the cry of a relatively small band of men and women who still cherished the ideals of the original ANC for bringing an end to apartheid. This group succeeded in making the South African government an international pariah.

However, the intransigence of successive apartheid regimes since 1948 and their unparalleled arrogance convinced many around the world that the only way to end apartheid was through the violent overthrow of the South African government. Thus, Umkhonto WeSizwe's (MK) call for an armed struggle against the minority white government found much support within the left in the West, the former Soviet block, as well as in some Asian, Latin American, and African countries. MK was offered military training facilities for its would-be guerrillas in several African countries and volunteer instructors from the then-Soviet Union offered their services. Once trained, guerrillas were equipped with military hardware, ranging from uniforms to surface-to-air missiles worth hundreds of millions of dollars.

In order to show the world that it was serious about warfare, MK signed the Geneva Convention on the treatment of prisoners of war, as well as the United Nations Declaration on Human Rights. The world was treated to a generous supply of information about the armed struggle which, like the armed struggles in Zimbabwe, Mozambique, Angola, and Guinnea Bisau would end in the defeat of the oppressive regime. In the process, "the world" conferred on the communist-led ANC the title of "sole, legitimate representative" of all black South Africans. This title not only awarded the communists with the moral high ground, but it also exempted the movement from criticism, let alone scrutiny of its internal workings. All eyes were on the evil apartheid regime and hardly anyone paid attention to what the communists were doing.

The ANC leadership gave the appearance of success in other areas as well. As the movement grew in stature, the leadership consolidated its power which, towards the end of the exile period in 1989, had become quite formidable. Indeed, one could speak of a government-in-waiting — just waiting to replace the Pretoria regime. But as we know, power can become insidiously dangerous and, in a very strange way, destroy the very people who wield it.

Somewhere towards the end of the 1960s the communist ANC leadership became intoxicated with power and embarked on a journey which has brought much grief to a great many South Africans.

Far from being committed to the liberation of the oppressed, this new communist-led ANC was interested only in power. The leadership became involved in criminal activity and corruption. A car theft ring within the movement was organized. Cars, especially Mercedes Benzes and BMWs, were stolen from South Africa and sold in other African countries.

Another department of the new communist ANC smuggled diamonds from Botswana and sold them on the international black market. Joe Modise, who took over as chief of staff after Joseph Slovo, was actually arrested for diamond smuggling in Botswana, and it took the intervention of Oliver Tambo, president of the communist ANC, to secure his release. The same leadership also got involved in the lucrative drug trade between India and South Africa. Mandrax, a potent illegal drug, which has the same effect as cocaine, is still smuggled from India through Zambia and Mozambique and sold in South Africa by the ANC.

Illicit dealings in arms and ivory also became part of the ordinary business of the ANC leadership. The large sums of money received were spent on expensive cars and luxurious homes, farms, jewelry, and travel. On the other hand, the small but steady flow of would-be freedom fighters which arrived in Botswana, Zambia, and Tanzania from South Africa had to live in conditions which ranged from spartan to inhuman. To deal with inevitable criticism and complaints, the leadership created and surrounded itself with a security force of South African criminals who were trained as agents in the then-Soviet Union and East Germany. The name of this force, which still operates inside and outside South Africa, is *MBOKODO*, which means "grinding stone" in both Xhosa and Zulu.

In the early 1970s, Angola, Mozambique, Namibia, and Zimbabwe were engaged in armed struggles which would eventually free them from colonial rule. The communist ANC was freeing no one. It was, instead, the only liberation movement which convinced the world that it was fighting an armed struggle but whose leadership never left the safety of international luxury hotels and conference rooms. The leadership never intended to launch a real armed struggle against South Africa. After all, the interminable rhetoric about an armed struggle was a very profitable business. The leadership never once thought that apartheid would end soon. ANC propaganda, broadcast from radio stations in Zambia, Ethiopia, and Tanzania did succeed in convincing many young black children in South Africa that the movement was actually fighting the South African Defense Force (SADF), though. And this led to tragedy.

South Africa's political landscape unexpectedly and dramatically changed in June 1976. Black students, mainly in the Johannesburg area, demonstrated peacefully, against being forced to study in Afrikaans, a language abhorrent to them. The terrified South African government responded with incredible force leaving more than one thousand dead and many more injured. Thousands of young black South Africans fled the country. Their aim was to go for military training and then return to overthrow the evil apartheid regime. They were driven by a burning passion for freedom and a conviction that only force would change apartheid. Almost all of them were in their teens — idealistic, committed, and unschooled in the treachery of politics. They risked everything for the sake of freedom. They were also joined by criminals and opportunists.

The majority of these youngsters traveled to Swaziland, Botswana, and Lesotho. There they were recruited either by the ANC or the Pan Africanist Congress. They were promised either further education or military training. Since most of them were still seething with anger at having seen their classmates and friends murdered in cold blood, most wanted to go for military training. This posed a major dilemma for the ANC leadership because the last thing they wanted was to fight a real liberation war in South Africa. However, the flight of large numbers of "refugees" from South Africa had a positive side as far as the leadership was concerned. Appeals for material aid were made to the same "international community" and the response was generous, to say the least. Most of the money went into the pockets of the ANC leadership, leaving the youngsters to live in destitute refugee camps.

The children and young relatives of the leadership, on the other hand, were sent to the best schools overseas or given important positions within the movement. Those who had no

THE AFRICAN NATIONAL CONGRESS 1912-1960

connections to the leadership were sent for military training. The would-be freedom fighters believed that after training they would be sent back to South Africa from Angola, Zimbabwe, Mozambique, and Namibia to fight for liberation. This was not to be. Upon completing training they were deployed instead in camps in Angola, Zambia, Tanzania, and Mozambique.

The new guerrillas soon complained about the lack of democracy within the movement, about corrupt leadership, inactivity, and unpleasant conditions within the camps, all of which led to low morale. They called for a conference which would restructure the movement and give it a new direction. The young and inexperienced guerrillas were out maneuvered.

In 1985, the conference they called for convened. The purpose was indeed to restructure the movement, but not in the democratic direction the young guerrillas had in mind.

At this unrepresentative conference held in Kabwe, Zambia, in June 1985, the executives of the ANC and SACP were merged, effectively making the two organizations one. Thus, the goal of the SACP of taking over the ANC which was announced in 1924 was reached in 1985. All those who still cherished the ideals of the original ANC resigned. I too resigned.

The liberal media never reported that in June 1985, Joseph Slovo, a Lithuanian and colonel in the KGB took over the ANC, and to this day, remains its leader. Mandela is a mere figurehead.

Kabwe saw the death of what was once a great black movement, the African National Congress. I am one of those who totally despise everything Joseph Slovo stands for.

I do not underestimate Slovo's enormous internal magnetic energy and his capacity to do evil. He is a brilliant tactician and has a great mind. Therein lies the danger. He has no equal in white South Africa. I have reason to believe that the only person Slovo is afraid of is Mangosuthu Buthelezi.

Despite silence from the liberal media, Joseph Slovo is working tirelessly to transform South Africa into a communist state. He is well on his way to achieving that goal. Who ever thought the National Party would one day be on the same side as the South African Communist Party? De Klerk and his National Party have now agreed that they will govern South Africa jointly with the communists. Thus, Slovo has scored yet another major victory.

The coalition between the ANC and the Communist Party has continued to strengthen since 1985. Three years ago, the communists tightened their grip on the ANC. The Johannesburg newspaper *Citizen* (July 8, 1991) reported the new arrangement: "The South African Communist Party totally dominated the elections to the National Executive Committee of the African National Congress at the weekend, with 37 of its members elected out of the 50 chosen."

A 65-year struggle was culminated in this terse comment. The communists are now poised to capture South Africa — the prize they have coveted for nearly a century.

After Joseph Slovo took control of the African National Congress, the organization took a brutal and ominous turn for the worse.

The Eyewitness Accounts of Torture Victims

Gordon Moshoeu —

Among the thousands who escaped from South Africa in 1976 was 21-year-old Gordon Moshoeu. This was his second time to experience state-sponsored brutality. At the tender age of 10, he saw his father gunned down by the South African police. He still does not know why. The events of June 16 and the following days convinced him that the only way to end apartheid in South Africa was through the military defeat of the South African army and police.

It is important to note that Gordon had never been politically active. His interests were education and soccer. He gave these up in order to avenge the brutal deaths of his father, classmates, and friends, and also to free his fellow countrymen.

Once Gordon and other young South Africans arrived in Botswana they were placed in protective custody. Some of the escapees were as young as nine years old. Here is Gordon's story:

"After a few days in protective custody, we were visited by representatives of the African National Congress, the Pan Africanist Congress, and the Black Consciousness Movement. Each group tried to recruit us for military training or further education. We were promised money, good food, clothes, and scholarships to overseas schools and universities. I decided to join the ANC. After a few weeks in Botswana, I was selected, together with 12 other South Africans, to go to Angola for military training.

"Our journey took us to the southern part of Angola, to a place called Katenga. For 18 months we were trained by Cubans in guerrilla warfare, sabotage, and demolition. After graduation I was sent to Bulgaria to study Marxism/Leninism.

"I returned to Angola in 1979 and was appointed commissar, which made me responsible for teaching Marxism/Leninism to the guerrillas who were stationed near Quibaxe in northern Angola. My superior held the rank of commander and was responsible for security at the camp. All together there were three camps in northern Angola. My first assignment was at Pango.

"After spending two months at Pango, I was moved to Fazenda, which was a camp for the so-called unruly elements. By this time there was growing discontent among the trained guerrillas. Many were disillusioned. They had come to Angola to train so that they could go back to South Africa and topple the apartheid regime militarily. They came to realize that the ANC leadership was not serious about fighting. The so-called "armed struggle" was nothing more than a ploy to raise large sums of money for the leadership. Conditions in the camps were miserable. On the other hand, the leadership lived very well. There were also charges of corruption and nepotism. The children and relatives of the leadership did not train as guerrillas. They were given scholarships to study at private schools and universities abroad.

"My last assignment as Commissar was at Camp 13 which housed approximately 1,300 guerrillas. This was the biggest camp.

"On January 7, 1981, commissars and commanders were summoned to Luanda, the capital of Angola, by Moses Mabida who was a top ANC official. In an address to the commissars and commanders, he charged that the guerrilla movement had been infiltrated by South African agents and spies. He gave orders to the security personnel that such elements had to be killed. The security personnel were young boys between 14 and 18 years. The speech was taped and played back to the inmates in the camps.

"There was a general uproar in the camps. The guerrillas were in effect hostages in the camps. Idleness led to anger and anger led to loss of confidence in what was essentially a corrupt leadership. I, of course, was also very angry.

"On January 13, I was arrested and taken to Quatro prison, a jail built by the ANC. I was thrown in jail by Andrew Masondo, another senior member of the ANC Executive. Young boys who did not even know me accused me of being a South African agent. I spent the next 18 months in solitary confinement where I was beaten and tortured by young boys who had been indoctrinated by the ANC leadership. All those who beat and tortured me were members of the Xhosa tribe.

"After 18 months I was moved to a cell with other inmates. We were subjected to long working days; food was scarce and bad; we were allowed one cup of water a day. The cups were made in China. We were not allowed any reading materials; there were no lights in the cells, nor were there any toilets. We were being brutalized by our own people, who were telling the world that they were fighting for our liberation and freedom.

"In 1982, the execution of inmates started. There were never any charges brought against anyone except to say the person was an "umdlwambe" (Xhosa for an enemy agent).

Torture was used to extract confessions. The walls of the torture chambers were splashed with blood and the floors were littered with human teeth. It was a ghastly sight. The stench from rotting pieces of human flesh was revolting. Both the days and nights were filled with the cries and groans of those being tortured or those suffering from wounds inflicted by their "liberators." Some of those who were subjected to sustained torture lost their minds and were sent to the ANC mental asylum in Tanzania, where they faced death from neglect. I must add here that some of the young security guards who were responsible for the torture also lost their minds and were similarly dumped in Tanzania near the town of Morogoro.

"In 1982, my mother sent my younger brother Gariel Paki Moshoeu to look for me in Botswana where she believed I was living with relatives. While in Botswana, he was recruited by the ANC and sent to Angola. I still do not know why, and I probably will never know, he was executed in 1983 by ANC firing squad together with 12 other recruits. I was only allowed one brief moment with him before his young life ended brutally. Those responsible for his execution were Andrew Masondo, Mzwandile Piliso and Mike Sandlwana.

"In 1984, things finally came to a head. Guerrillas could no longer stomach the indiscriminate arrests, torture, and cold-blooded murder of compatriots. Further, they were tired of fighting against UNITA in Angola and could not understand why they were not being sent to South Africa to liberate their own people. These matters could not be discussed with the ANC leadership, since anyone who asked questions was declared an agent of the enemy, arrested, tortured, and even murdered. The guerrillas, therefore, had no alternative but to mutiny. As was to be expected, the mutiny was brutally put down. The National Executive Council of the ANC and the South African Communist Party bear full responsibility for all the murders that followed.

"I survived and finally made my way to the United States through the help of friends."

Sipho Amos Laliso —

Sipho Amos Laliso was imprisoned in a camp called Viana in Angola in 1983. Chris Hani and Joe Modise decided that he and others should be moved to northern Angola to a camp called Pango. The notorious Andrew Masonda was there. Sipho witnessed the execution of five inmates; Dihuba, Gibson, Lungile, Mzi, and Sticks. He was one of those forced to dig their graves with his bare hands. He was finally moved to Quatro. He was tortured and told to confess that he was a spy. In 1990, he was smuggled to Uganda for further torture. He was released on August 16, 1991, with the title "most notorious enemy agent." He had spent eight years in ANC prisons.

Abeod M. Laka —

Abeod M. Laka escaped from South Africa in 1986 with the intention of finishing his studies. In Lusaka he was told to write his autobiography. He was then arrested and sent to the ANC's rehabilitation center, where he was beaten with fists, sticks, and an electric cable until he admitted he was a spy. His prison mate was Patrick Hlongwane. From Lusaka he was sent to Quatro in northern Angola, where he shared a four-by-four-meter cell with 12 inmates. They existed on beans, porridge, and half-cooked rice; there was no medical attention available; water was rationed to one cup a day and he was subjected to daily beatings and hard labor. He was transferred to Uganda where he was released on August 16, 1991, and was dubbed "most notorious enemy agent." He spent five years in ANC prisons.

Mandla Mapu —

Mandla Mapu escaped from South Africa in 1986. In Botswana he was told to write his autobiography and after that he was sent to Angola — first to Viana and then Quatro. He was forced to confess that he was a spy and that he had slept with Winnie Mandela. For five months he was in solitary confinement and was tortured daily by a man called Griffith.

Everyone in the camp was given a new name. His was Mthunzi Tsikila and his derogatory name was Bacon. Rats were put on his head. His body was smeared with fish oil and he was covered with red ants which bit him. Everyone was beaten daily at Quatro. Chris Hani ordered his transfer to Uganda, where he was finally released on August 16, 1991, after being labeled "most notorious enemy agent." He spent five years in ANC prisons.

Siphowe Bethuel Lombo —

In January 1986, Siphiwe Bethuel Lombo was asked to drive two friends across the border to Botswana. They were being harassed by the South African Security Police. At the time he was working for Sanlam Insurance Company as a Group Scheme Advisor. In Botswana, ANC functionaries asked him to work with their underground structures once he returned to South Africa. When he refused, they asked him to travel to Lusaka to discuss the matter with Oliver Tambo, the ANC president. He agreed.

Siphiwe says, "That was my grievous mistake." From Lusaka, he was sent to Tanzania to meet Alfred Nzo, then general secretary of the ANC. In Tanzania, the ANC arrested him, tied him to a tree, and beat him with bicycle chains and barbed wire until he was unconscious. He was returned to Lusaka, where, after being forced to write his autobiography, was made to dig his own grave and to stand upright in it as it was filled with soil. By the time he was covered up to his chest, he was short of breath and he fainted. When he regained consciousness, he was in his cell.

"This was done to me," Siphiwe says, "because MBOKODO, the security branch of the ANC accused me of being a senior official of the South African government's National Intelligence Service." In other words, he was accused of being a spy for the South African government. Siphiwe says, "Alfred Nzo demanded that I surrender all the necessary information that they wanted before it was too late for me."

He continues:

"From Lusaka, I was sent to Angola to a prison called Novo Stalacao and placed in special 'death row cells.' My cell was next to that of Captain Du Toit. I went on a hunger strike because I did not understand why I was kept in prison.

"My next destination was Quatro, the ANC's most notorious camp.

"There I was placed in solitary confinement for six months, where I was tortured daily in an effort to force me to admit that I was an enemy agent. People who interrogated and tortured me included Chris Hani, Ronnie Kasrils, Joe Nhlanhla, two Soviets — one by the name of Boris and another one who did not mention his name. Others included the commander of the camp, Professor Griffith Siboni; the camp commissar, Dan Mashingo; Chief of Staff Morgan; the chief of logistics, and Bob, the most notorious of them all.

"When the ANC was expelled from Angola in 1989, we were transferred to Uganda. Before that, we were made to make a video at gun point. In the video we 'confessed' that we were spies. I was released from the dungeons of the ANC on August 14, 1991.

"In South Africa, the ANC has tried to paint us as the 'most notorious enemy agents' so that people in the townships can kill us. The atrocities committed by the ANC must be investigated."

Skekana Alpheus Kheswa —

Skekana Alpheus Kheswa left South Africa in 1986 because the South African Security Police were about to arrest him for his pro-ANC activities. He traveled to Botswana where he was made to write his autobiography. From Botswana the ANC took him to Zambia and on to Tanzania, where he committed the fatal mistake of clashing with MBOKODO. He was accused of being an enemy agent and when he sought refuge at the United Nations High Commission for Refugees, he was sent back to the ANC. There his torture began. He was beaten with sticks and iron rods and forced to 'confess' that he was an agent of the South African government. He was also accused of killing a number of ANC officials.

From Tanzania, he was taken to Angola. He ended up in Quatro, where beatings with barbed wire, bicycle chains, and iron rods were commonplace. He personally witnessed the execution by firing squad of 44 Quatro inmates. They were accused of being South African spies.

Just the Tip of the Iceberg

These horror stories are but a small sample of the sad tales told by the survivors of the ANC "military" camps. It is hard to believe that those who claimed to be liberators could treat their own members in a manner which was infinitely worse than that of their oppressors. It is even harder to believe when one remembers that the African National Congress is revered around the world as an organization that is dedicated to fighting racism and oppression in South Africa; as one that respects human rights and human dignity; as one that is striving to establish democracy and freedom for all the citizens of South Africa. To associate such an organization and its leadership with concentration camps is viewed as sacrilege by the uninformed.

The international image of the ANC leadership as selfless martyrs who have suffered enormous persecution while practicing fairness, tolerance, and democracy within their own ranks is beginning to unravel. This despite strenuous media efforts to conceal the heinous atrocities of the ANC. Still, one truth can destroy a thousand lies. And to this ideal we must cling in our time of need.

Former guerrillas who have recently returned to South Africa after many years of exile give an account of their treatment at the hands of the ANC leadership which numbs the mind. They report arrests by the ANC security (MBOKODO), imprisonment without trial, torture, murder, and executions. Yet, one of the saddest truths associated with these events is that this tortuous, murderous band of criminals is the organization which America supports with tens of millions of dollars.

The *New York Times* (August 31, 1993) acknowledged that other sources have reported these same facts concerning torture and death in the ANC camps:

> "The commission report ... found that from the late 1970's until 1991 suspected spies and dissidents were imprisoned for up to eight years without any hearing, beaten to extract confessions, and tortured during their confinement. The commission listed cases of prisoners executed by firing squads for taking part in mutinies, or beaten to death for infractions of military discipline, or dead of malaria and other conditions in detention."

The survivors speak of being arrested in Zambia, Botswana, Tanzania, Angola, Uganda, and Mozambique. They were placed in camps where they were stripped naked and beaten with electric wire; they were given clothing infested with lice; they were given one cup of water a day; they were given half-cooked food, or no food at all; they were crammed into small cells with little ventilation, little light, and no toilet facilities.

They speak of being given no medical attention — of lying in their own vomit and their own excreta. They detail the methods of torture used by the ANC on their own dissident members. They were forced to dig graves with their bare hands for their murdered or executed colleagues. They were also forced to make false confessions. They witnessed executions by firing squads and young women who were raped, sodomized, and then kicked to death. Some of their friends were forced to eat their own excreta, others were burned alive. Still others were left hanging from trees for days on end.

At the most notorious of the prison camp — Quatro, which is north of Luanda in Angola — the floor of one of the torture chambers was covered with human teeth. The walls and floors were splattered with human blood and pieces of human flesh. The cells had a permanent nauseating stench which came from untreated, festering wounds. Virtually none of the women who became pregnant knew who fathered their babies. They were, after all, property of the movement. The survivors speak of those who lost their minds as a result of being tortured, and those who lost them because they could no longer cope with the guilt of deliberately causing unspeakable human suffering. Most of the rank and file in MBOKODO were teenagers forced to do the dirty work of an evil leadership.

Cover-up and Denial

The silence concerning these horrific events is deafening; the Clinton Administration, the United Nations, the Organization of African Unity, TransAfrica, the Congressional Black Caucus, the Lawyers for Human Rights, Jesse Jackson, and a multitude of other spokesmen and organizations have all remained conspicuously closed-mouthed about the torture, mayhem, suffering, and murder perpetrated by members and officials of the African National Congress.

Presently, the ANC is still using its MBOKODO inside South Africa to suppress the publication of what is clearly the most sordid story in the history of South Africa. Remember that these barbaric acts were committed by people who claim to be liberators and who committed them against their own people. The victims who are speaking out do so at great risk to themselves and their loved ones. At least two former ANC prisoners, Sipho Phungulwa and Shongwe, have already been assassinated in South Africa — apparently by MBOKODO. The survivors of the camps have organized themselves into committees. It is through their personal stories as well as those of other ANC prisoners that we are allowed a glimpse into what must go down in history as the greatest evil ever committed in the name of liberation.

Most of those who were brutally murdered and buried in mass graves or left to be eaten by wild animals will probably remain anonymous forever. But some left behind photographs and names and some of the survivors know how they were murdered.

This gruesome story not only numbs the human senses, it raises frightening and ominous questions about the future of South Africa. Most of the victims of ANC inhumanity were in their teens and early twenties. Most of them were loyal members of the ANC. They wanted to fight for the liberation of their people and country when they were lured into the ANC death camps. One cannot help but ask: If the ANC leadership can treat its own people so savagely, what will it do to its declared enemies such as Inkatha, Bophuthatswana, Ciskei, and the non-communists who reject the ANC's hegemony? Can people who display absolute disregard for human rights, even among their own members, ever be trusted with power? What will stop these savages from carrying out mass murders among their opponents, especially Christians, in the name of ideological cleansing?

Why has the "international community" remained silent for so long and shown no interest in an issue which has potentially deadly consequences for the future of South Africa?

Action must be taken and taken without further delay. The South African government, the South African people, and the international organizations claiming to be the promoters of human rights, must bring the evil-doers to the bar of justice.

The South African government must acknowledge the atrocities in the ANC camps immediately. The government must admit these crimes were committed by South Africans against South Africans. Charges must be brought in South African courts against those who were personally responsible for the hideous crimes carried out by members of the African National Congress and the South African Communist Party. Charges must be brought against these two organizations as well, since the systematic nature of the brutality indicates central, organized planning.

Initially, the de Klerk government, knowing these charges are true, intended to prosecute the perpetrators. However, under pressure from the ANC, the government caved in and signed an accord granting amnesty to the criminals. *Facts on File* (August 15, 1991) reported:

"Under the accord, blanket amnesty would be extended for all political offenses committed in South Africa or in exile through Oct. 8, 1990. Previously, the government had demanded that the repatriation of exiles be conducted on a case by case basis. Those charged with common crimes would not benefit from the offer, nor would political prisoners in South African jails.... The amnesty was one of the ANC's demands for renewing negotiations with the government on a new constitution."

Over 20,000 communist-ANC terrorists were let back into the country through the amnesty that President de Klerk signed. They came back with their arms, which included AK-47s, limpet mines, grenades, and rocket launchers. Also, over 15,000 common criminals were released from South African jails.

These events account for the great increase in violence in South Africa over the past three years. More than 10,000 innocent civilians have lost their lives. No two men have been more responsible for this than Nelson Mandela and F.W. de Klerk. Yet in spite of all this, in 1993 America has awarded them the Medal of Freedom and Sweden has astonishingly given them the Nobel Prize for Peace.

The callous attempts by the West to wink at these heinous crimes and to present Mandela and de Klerk as paragons of moral virtue, must not be allowed to succeed. Both the survivors and relatives of those who were brutally murdered must press charges. They are entitled to damages from the individuals responsible, and also from the ANC and SACP. Both organizations have hundreds of millions of dollars in assets. They must be forced to pay compensation. The magnitude of the hideous crimes they committed against defenseless South Africans is so great that there can be no pardon. Justice must be served.

Mandela has been forced to admit that ANC comrades did indeed commit these crimes. After details of the atrocities surfaced, the ANC appointed its own commission to investigate the charges. Their findings were reported in the *New York Times* (August 24, 1993):

> "The African National Congress published an independent report today detailing torture and death in its own military camps in the years of guerilla war against apartheid. The report named accused torturers, some of whom still hold posts in the congress's security apparatus, and said the congress should pay reparations to surviving victims."

Despite the charges and the admissions, Mandela and the ANC adamantly refuse to even discipline the perpetrators. Again, quoting from the *New York Times* (August 31, 1993):

> "The African National Congress issued a blanket apology today for torture, executions and other abuses committed in its war against apartheid, but said it would not punish past human rights violators or pay compensation to the victims.
>
> "Responding to an independent report that detailed abuses and cited men who still hold positions in the organization, Nelson Mandela, the president of the congress, said it would be unfair to discipline those accused within the anti-apartheid movement when officials who committed atrocities in support of apartheid remain free."

Mandela puts forth the weakest of arguments; Because injustice exists elsewhere, we can't administer justice ourselves. What would be the implications of such thinking in an ANC government? By Mandela's reasoning an ANC government would be justified in carrying out similar brutalities as long as political opponents existed.

On the international front, we must bear in mind that these crimes were committed by South Africans in foreign lands. Survivors claim that there was collaboration by the ANC/SACP with certain governments. Some of the survivors were actually held in national jails and guarded by national soldiers. Some of the South African prisoners were apparently executed by national soldiers. The questions are:

- How much did the governments of Botswana, Mozambique, Zambia, Angola, Tanzania, Uganda, and South Africa know about these ritual murders?
- How was it possible for the ANC/SACP's prisoners to be flown from one African country to another? Who issued the false passports? Why were they honored by the country of destination?
- How true are the claims that the United Nations High Commission for Refugees in the above-mentioned countries collaborated with the ANC/SACP and, instead of providing refuge for the persecuted, actually sent them back to the camps where death awaited them?
- Even as the inmates of the death camps starved, MBOKODO was well-fed. The food for the torturers and murderers came from Sweden, according to the testimony of the survivors. What was Sweden's role in the torture and murder of young, innocent, black South Africans? What did authorities in Stockholm know about what was going on in Quatro?
- What did Western governments know? The United States has a sophisticated information-gathering network. What did Washington know about the atrocities? Why the silence?

An independent international commission of inquiry must be set up to investigate the ANC's reign of terror in its entirety. If other countries are found to have aided the Stalinist ANC/SACP, directly or indirectly, the victims and their relatives must be compensated.

The governments of Angola, Botswana, Mozambique, Tanzania, Uganda, and Zambia must volunteer information concerning the atrocities committed by the ANC/SACP in their countries. Failing this, these countries must be expelled from all international bodies.

Murder and Mayhem Revisited

Since the 1960s, African dictators have murdered millions of their own people with impunity. The world has turned a deaf ear to the cries of agony and a blind eye to unspeakable suffering. As we move to the 21st century, African dictators and would-be dictators must be taught that the age of barbarism is over.

It is important to remember that the murderers within the ranks of the ANC/SACP are poised to participate in the next South African government. If that happens, the outcome would be an imponderable disaster. That must be prevented at all cost.

The following are responsible for the ANC murder camps. As members of the ANC's National Executive Committee, they were responsible for all the activities of their organization, including the atrocities in their camps. The names are arranged in alphabetical order.

Stephen Dlamini	Florence Mophosho
Chris Hani	Anthony Mongalo
Paulo Jordan	Joe Nhlanhla
Moses Mabhida	John Nkadimeng
Mac Maharaj	Aziz Pahad
Simon Makana	Mzwai Piliso
Johnny Makatini	Reg September
Cassius Make	Gertrude Shope
Robert Manci	Sizakele Sigxashe
Thabo Mbeki	Joseph Slovo (Joe)
Francis Meli	James Stuart
Joe Modise	Dan Tloome
Ruth Mombati	Jacob Zuma

Chapter 3

Nelson Mandela

Observers of the South African scene are unanimous in describing February 1990, as a watershed in South African political history. On the second day of that month, President F.W. de Klerk stunned friend and foe alike, when he announced the unbanning of the African National Congress (ANC), the Pan Africanist Congress (PAC), the South African Communist Party (SACP), and many other banned organizations. It is widely believed that de Klerk's announcement, which insinuated the future of South Africa is to be negotiated by all interested parties, regardless of race and political affiliation, marks the beginning to the end of apartheid. De Klerk has signaled the National Party government is willing to negotiate itself out of power. For the first time in the more than 300-year history of South Africa, the possibility of establishing a nonracial democracy in the country exists.

For thousands of South Africans, the announcement also meant an end to exile. Those who had left South Africa for strictly political reasons, could now return without fear of either persecution or prosecution.

Reactions to de Klerk's announcement were as contradictory as everything else about South Africa. There were those who praised him for the bold and realistic steps he had taken. Others saw his actions as a ploy designed to entrench white supremacy, albeit in a new guise. Others cried, "Treason." Still others were simply dumbfounded.

But the high drama was yet to come — a little more than a week later. On February 11, Nelson Mandela was released from "prison." In actual fact, he spent the last four years of his prison term outside prison in Cape Town. From 1986, he engaged in extensive and intensive negotiations with the South African government. I firmly believe it was during those discussions that agreement on the future of South Africa was surreptitiously reached between the government and Mandela.

In 1964, Mandela and seven others had been sentenced to life imprisonment for plotting the violent overthrow of the South African government. The communists had chosen Mandela to carry their water, and the international media worked tirelessly to build him into a figure of mythical proportions. During the last decade South Africans of all races and from all walks of life made concerted efforts to secure his release and the release of all political prisoners. The call was joined by people and governments all over the world.

When Mandela was finally released from prison, excitement and expectations ran high in many quarters of South Africa. The international media converged on South Africa to record the historic event and millions of television viewers from around the world sat glued to their sets and watched. I was among them.

As I watched him stride towards freedom, I felt as though every South African, black and white, was beginning a long journey out of prison to a new, free South Africa. From the safety of exile in Atlanta, I began to reflect on my own involvement with the ANC which began literally in infancy.

I first met Nelson Mandela in 1952 in Durban, my hometown, during one of the defiance campaigns. He was in the company of local ANC leaders. I later found out more about him from those who knew him well.

Mandela's Communist Past

In ANC circles it was a well known fact that Mandela was a communist. When he became a founding member of the ANC's Youth League (ANCYL) in 1943, he became part of the Marxist group which opposed the Christian group. Mandela's group accused the ANC leadership of being enslaved by a "dying order of pseudo-liberalism and conservatism, of appeasement and compromise." They disparagingly referred to the ANC leadership as "the old guard."

The ANCYL did not believe in peaceful change. They wanted the violent overthrow of the South African government. They wanted revolution. That is one reason why Anton Lembede, the first president of the ANCYL, called Mandela an opportunist who could not be trusted.

The communist wing of the ANCYL greeted the banning of the ANC in 1960 with euphoria. The South African government had offered them the opportunity the Christian wing of the ANC had denied them for decades — the right to reject nonviolence and replace it with armed struggle. Mandela, it will be recalled, became the first commander of Umkhonto WeSizwe (MK). The following is how the leaders of MK were described at their trial in 1963. Mandela, who was the commander of this terrorist group, was the first accused.

> "The accused deliberately and maliciously plotted and engineered the commission of acts of violence and destruction throughout the country.... The planned purpose was to bring about in the Republic of South Africa chaos, disorder, and turmoil which would be aggravated, according to their plan, by the operation of thousands of trained guerrilla warfare units deployed throughout the country at various vantage points. These would be joined in the various areas by local inhabitants as well as specially selected men posted at such areas. Their combined operations were planned to lead to confusion, violent insurrection, and rebellion, followed, at the appropriate juncture, by an armed invasion of the country by military units of foreign powers." (*A History of Communism in South Africa*:

Henry R. Pike. Christian Mission International, Pretoria 1985. p. 388.)

Before being sent to prison for life, Mandela wrote a long essay entitled: "How to be a Good Communist." (See appendix A.) He revealed his true self in that volume:

"The aim is to change the present world into a Communist world where there will be no exploiters and exploited, no oppressor and oppressed, no rich and poor. (p.1)

"Under a Communist Party Government, South Africa will become a land of milk and honey. Political, economic and social rights will cease to be enjoyed by whites only. They will be shared equally by whites and non-whites. There will be no unemployment, starvation and disease. Workers will earn decent wages; transport will be cheap and education free. There will be no Pass Laws, no influx control, no police raids for passes and poll tax, and Africans, Europeans, Coloureds and Indians will live in racial peace and perfect equality. (p.3)

"Without a hard, bitter and long struggle against capitalism and exploitation, there can be no Communist world. The cause of Communism is the greatest cause in the history of mankind because it seeks to remove from society all forms of oppression and exploitation, to liberate mankind and to ensure peace and prosperity to all. (p.27.)

"We test a Communist Party member's loyalty to the Party, to the revolution and the Communist cause by the manner in which he absolutely subordinates his interests to those of the Communist Party.... In the Party our members should not have personal aims independent of the Party's interests.... A member of our Party is no longer just an ordinary person. He is a conscious vanguard fighter of the working class." (pp.30, 31, 34.)

We in the ANC, therefore, knew that Mandela was a communist. However, after he had served 15 years of his life sentence, many felt it was time for him to be released on humanitarian grounds. I felt that way too. I thought that he had changed; that he was old and would not have the energy or inclination to pursue his earlier plans of destruction and murder. So, it was reasonable for Mandela to be released.

Preparations for Mandela's Release

In 1978 I wrote a song entitled *"Qinisela Mandela"* — Persevere Mandela — we will secure your release from prison. The song was recorded by the South African Freedom Singers and was distributed worldwide through anti-apartheid organizations.

Even though I resigned from the ANC in 1985, I was overjoyed to see Mandela walk out of prison that fateful day in February 1990. The so-called armed struggle had been a dismal failure. Nonviolent pressure had secured Mandela's release.

Like many South Africans, I wondered what Mandela would do after gaining his freedom. My joy at seeing him released was, therefore, accompanied by a deep sense of apprehension, perhaps even anxiety.

The government of South Africa had ignored calls for Mandela's release, insisting that since he was sent to prison for espousing violence, he must renounce violence before he could be released. Mandela steadfastly refused. The government tried to isolate Mandela and his ANC, seeking instead to negotiate a settlement of apartheid with black leaders who rejected the use of violence to achieve political goals. One such leader is Chief Mangosuthu Buthelezi who is based in Natal on the east coast of South Africa. This is the ancestral home of the Zulus.

Chief Buthelezi is himself a former member of the ANC.

Since the banning of the ANC in 1960, no other black political leader in South Africa has taken a more principled position than Buthelezi in his dealings with the South African government. Three tribes or national groups had accepted cutting off links with South Africa and becoming black independent states. These were the Xhosa — Mandela's people — the Venda, and the Tswana. The first such homeland, as these states became known, was the Transkei, founded in 1976 by the Xhosa. Those who accepted breaking away from South

Africa to form a sovereign state or republic were Mandela's cousins — Kaiser and George Matanzima. They and their successors were so corrupt that the Transkei, like many other African states, is now a military dictatorship. The Ciskei, another Xhosa Republic, which severed ties with South Africa, also has a military government. The civilian government was overthrown in a bloody coup in 1989. The ANC never vilified the Xhosa republics of the Transkei and the Ciskei. When Bophuthatswana and Venda were established, the ANC refrained from verbally attacking the leadership of these two homelands. Chief Buthelezi and the Zulus chose to stay a part of South Africa.

The South African government, whose grand apartheid plan envisaged ten black sovereign states and one white super state, tried its best to force the Zulus to sever ties with South Africa and become an independent state. The Zulus are the largest black ethnic group in South Africa, numbering nine million. If they had accepted independence, apartheid would have succeeded in isolating blacks and the course of South African history would have completely changed.

In 1974, Chief Buthelezi and other former ANC members formed *Inkatha Yenkululeko Yesizwe* (Inkatha). "Inkatha" is a grass coil worn by women on their heads to help them bear a heavy burden. Inkatha Yenkululeko Yesizwe, therefore, means a movement which shoulders the burden of liberating the nation. The movement was established to fight the grand designs of Pretoria. Through Inkatha, with its then-two-million members, Chief Buthelezi was able to prevent the South African government from creating and collaborating with Zulu puppets who would accept independence. He was able to establish a formidable political constituency which Pretoria could not ignore. He filled the vacuum created by the banning of the ANC. He withstood enormous pressure to negotiate a new political dispensation for South Africa by insisting that negotiations could take place only after the unbanning of the ANC and PAC and the release of Mandela and all political prisoners. He earned the wrath of the ANC when he refused to allow Inkatha to join the so-called armed struggle and when he opposed economic sanctions.

Buthelezi refused to be part of the armed struggle for several reasons. First, the ANC had never decided to launch an armed struggle. Mandela and a few blacks in Johannesburg who had become tools of the South African Communist Party made that decision. Second, it would have been suicide to launch an armed struggle against South African military forces without proper planning. Third, no other group in the entire continent of Africa had lost more men by fighting than the Zulus.

The Zulus are not afraid of war, but they are not suicidal, either. They are the only nation in Africa which has the distinction of ever defeating the British — even though they were armed with spears while the British had guns.

MK knew that without the participation of the Zulus in an armed struggle, the whole effort was doomed to failure. MK, therefore, mounted an international campaign to discredit Buthelezi and Inkatha. Inside South Africa, they heaped insults on him, portraying him and the Zulu people as collaborators and enemies of freedom. They targeted Buthelezi for assassination. MK also started a reign of terror in black townships, particularly in Natal, where Zulu Inkatha members were murdered and their houses burned.

In spite of this, Buthelezi communicated with Mandela while he was in prison and explained in detail what he was trying to accomplish. Mandela was appreciative and supportive.

During Mandela's long imprisonment, other black organizations were formed in South Africa. These included the Black Consciousness Movement (BCM), Inkatha Yenkululeko Yesizwe (Inkatha), the United Democratic Front (UDF), and the Azania People's Organization (AZAPO). New leaders emerged. Among the better known were Chief Mangosuthu Buthelezi and Steve Biko. These groups and many others saw in Mandela a unifying symbol of their struggle for freedom and justice as did the foreign media much later. There were many who believed that his absence from the turbulent political scene, factional politics, and the power struggles qualified him to be the undisputed national leader of all black South Africans and indeed, eventually all South Africans. People from different backgrounds saw no distinction between Mandela the man and Mandela the symbol. Hopes were high that upon his release, Mandela would see the futility of the so-called armed struggle which was causing havoc and anarchy in black communities. Many were convinced that he would be a man of peace and that he would use the considerable status conferred on him by the international media to end hostilities and bloodshed, that he would be a force for reconciliation.

This was a strongly held view even in international circles. South Africans were convinced that, as a respected father figure, he would succeed in getting their children back to school to prepare themselves for the post-apartheid tasks. They thought he was the only person who could reestablish discipline in their disoriented children and youth. Leaders assumed that he would bring together the warring political and tribal factions and head a united delegation to a constitutional conference which would produce a just constitution for South Africa. They saw him as the father and architect for the New South Africa. They forgot his criminal past and were willing to give him a second chance.

Many believed his release would bring the end of the economic misery caused by sanctions. South Africa's economic isolation would end; international banks would give loans; the economy would expand and grow. People, especially blacks hit hardest by sanctions, would find employment and be able to afford better housing and health care. Crime would therefore diminish and life in the black townships would eventually return to normal. They equated Mandela's release with the dawn of a magical new day in South Africa.

There were others whose main concern was whether he would break with his communist past. I shared this concern and I wondered whether he had grown and matured in prison or whether he was still given to the blind ambition and reckless opportunism evidenced by his decision to launch the so-called armed struggle in 1961.

By the time Mandela was released, communism was crumbling in Eastern Europe. It seemed reasonable to assume he would recognize communism as a fraud. Many also wondered how he would handle his wife Winnie who, during his imprisonment, had become not just a disgrace to the struggle for liberation, but a formidable terrorist. The burning question was: "Had Mandela, who was sentenced to life imprisonment for criminal activities, repented and grown, or was he coming out of prison a worse criminal than before?"

An Unrepentent Mandela

A few hours after his release, he stood on the steps of Cape Town City Hall and addressed a crowd estimated at 500,000. The nagging questions I and many others had were answered. First, his podium was draped in the Communist Party flag, not the flag of the ANC. Second, he declared:

> "I salute combatants of Umkhonto WeSizwe; I salute the South African Communist Party for its sterling contribution to the struggle for democracy, I salute the memory of great communists like Moses Katane, Yusuf Dadoo, Bram Fischer and Moses Mabida. Your memory will be cherished for generations to come. I salute General Secretary (of the South African Communist Party) Joe Slovo, one of our finest patriots. We are heartened by the fact that the alliance between ourselves and the Party remains as strong as it always was."

My hopes were shattered.

Mandela had saluted by name hard-core Stalinist members of the South African Communist Party. Just how the South African Communist Party has made "a sterling contribution to the struggle for democracy" is a riddle no human brain can handle.

I was also shocked to hear him say nothing had changed in the 27 years he was in prison. To me, this suggested incredible arrogance. He implied that no one had done anything in his absence, that he was the only one who could affect change in South Africa. His call for continued armed struggle dismayed all those who knew so well that the armed struggle was destroying blacks, without advancing their cause.

After almost 30 years of armed struggle, his guerrillas did not control one square inch of South African soil, but they had unleashed a reign of terror in black areas. His listeners knew that the superbly armed South African government could never be brought down violently. The people were not waiting for a warrior. They awaited the man who could lead them to peace. More than anything, they needed a spiritual leader.

Men and women who had lost their jobs, who had families to feed, the poor, the hungry, the sick were dismayed to hear Mandela call for more sanctions that day. For these people, sanctions simply meant more unnecessary suffering.

In a letter to Buthelezi, dated February 3, 1989, written from Victor Verster prison near Cape Town, Mandela stated:

> "Obviously, my fervent hope is to see, in due course, the restoration of the cordial relations which existed between you and Oliver Tambo, and between the two organizations in the seventies. The most challenging task facing the leadership today is that of national unity. At no other time in our history has it become so crucial for our young people to speak with one voice, and to pool their efforts."

For Buthelezi and millions of other black South Africans, Mandela's first speech after his release was the greatest disappointment of their lives. Mandela the man could not, and did not, live up to Mandela the symbol. Perhaps when he said nothing had changed he meant that he had not changed. He was a "loyal" and "disciplined" member of the ANC, a strong ally of the South African Communist Party. All blacks were to line up behind the ANC/SACP alliance or face the consequences.

Black South Africans were in for yet another shock. According to black South African cultures, a person who has been away for a period of time does not immediately give long speeches upon his return. To do so is to show disrespect and arrogance. The real leader listens to his or her followers before speaking. People therefore expected Mandela's speech on the steps of Cape Town City Hall to be a expression of gratitude to all South Africans and to people all over the world for their support. They expected him to call for unity of purpose, discipline, and dedicated hard work for a new South Africa. They expected to hear him dedicate himself to working tirelessly for peace. They expected him to consult others. They expected a statesman. Instead, they got an aging revolutionary who was full of aged rhetoric.

If Mandela had honored his cultural roots, he would have spent the first few months listening to his people, all of them, not just the ANC and the communists. He would have listened to students, trade unionists, academics, business people, the unemployed, the poor, the sick, the suffering, the well-to-do, the police, soldiers, orphans, widows, and widowers. He would have listened to blacks, whites, coloreds, and Indians. He would have traveled across South Africa, to the townships, the suburbs, the villages, and the cities. He would have visited the areas devastated by violence, particularly Natal. He would have met leaders, particularly other black leaders, including those of all the homelands. He would have sought counsel from people older than himself. In doing these things, he would have followed a wise and tested African tradition. Instead, Mandela limited himself to like-minded advisors. He canceled multiple appointments with Chief Mangosuthu Buthelezi, who had been a strong supporter during his incarceration.

Within weeks of his release, Mandela announced that an ANC/SACP Alliance government would nationalize the mines, banks, and other key industries. This amazed, threatened, or frightened many, especially because it came in the wake of the fall of communism in Eastern Europe, where nationalization had failed miserably. Some began to question Mandela's state of mind. Others concluded he was out of touch. Others felt he was a tool of the radical and irresponsible elements within the ANC/SACP Alliance. The numbers of those who doubted his ability to make positive contributions to a new South Africa increased dramatically.

It was not long before his influence was put to the test. At a rally at the black township of Soweto in Johannesburg he urged students to return to their schools and learn. Some of those in his audience actually shouted back: "You go back to prison." Many of the youngsters who went to the rally wearing Mandela t-shirts bearing the imprint of Mandela's head, used knives to cut out the head and threw it away in disgust. They refused to go back to school. His comrades had told them to chose revolution over education. Because he had not taken the time to talk with them and listen, he was unaware of what was on their minds.

During Mandela's time in prison, Winnie had surrounded herself with a band of thugs she called the Mandela Football Club. Instead of playing football, these guys terrorized neighborhoods and fought running battles with students. The students remember vividly that one of their number, Stompie Moeketsi Seipei, was beaten in Winnie's house in 1989. His partly decomposed body was found in a playing field. Most people in Soweto feel that Winnie is culpable in the death of Stompie. Because Mandela defended his wife after his release, many school-age South Africans have lost whatever respect they had for him.

When Mandela went to Durban to address his supporters, he called on them to end their violence and throw their knives, pangas, and guns into the sea. They laughed at him. There was a glaring contradiction between his avowed support for armed struggle and his calling for arms to be thrown into the sea. Some wondered aloud whether the old man was getting senile.

Far from heeding his call, they intensified the "armed struggle," sentencing hundreds of blacks, including innocent women and children, to death. Since Mandela's release, black-on-black violence has intensified. His inflammatory speeches add fuel to the fire, as did his initial refusal to meet with Chief Mangosuthu Buthelezi. Mandela the knight has become Mandela the nightmare.

De Klerk freed Mandela from the infamous Robben Island, but Mandela is incapable of releasing himself from the prison of a failed and discredited ideology: communism.

Taking the Moral Low Road

Since his release, Mandela has travelled extensively in Africa, Europe, the Americas, and Asia. He must have seen incredible poverty and devastation in African countries and great progress and wealth in Europe and America. It should be clear to him by now that there is a real First World and a real Third World. Yet, wherever he goes, he calls for sanctions against South Africa. These sanctions have caused more than 50 percent unemployment among black adults and 80 percent among black youth. He should know, if he has any sense at all, that poverty contributes not just to unnecessary suffering, but leads directly to crime and violence.

As president of the ANC, Mandela leads a Stalinist "liberation movement" that is a front for the South African Communist Party. To this day, the ANC has persistently refused to renounce violence as a means to political goals. Instead, the organization maintains its private army — MK. Why should young people heed his call for peace?

The ANC refuses to surrender its large stockpiles of sophisticated weapons hidden in various parts of South Africa, and continues to recruit young black South Africans who are sent for military training in Cuba and even Libya, a country the United States accuses of financing international terrorism. The ANC's official commitment to violence translates into the ongoing senseless and brutal killings in the black townships, despite the signing of various peace accords.

During his visit to the United States in June 1990, Mandela expressed admiration for Yasser Arafat, Fidel Castro, and Moammar Gadhafi. He viewed those three as role models and applauds them whenever able. Cuban exiles in Miami were so incensed that Mandela was denied the key to that city.

More important, however, are Mandela's remarks during an official visit to Cuba in July 1991. During that highly publicized trip, Mandela went out of his way, not only to praise Fidel Castro's human rights record, but to denounce Cuban exiles and other critics of Cuba's grotesque policies. Mandela sent shock waves throughout the world when he declared that the disastrous Cuban revolution is a "model for South Africa."

These and other reckless pronouncements show him to be a dangerous opportunist. He supported Sadam Hussein's invasion of Kuwait. While on a visit to Iran in July 1992, he praised the Islamic revolution and, in remarks echoing his Cuban speech, declared the Islamic Revolution to be a model for Africa. One wonders which failed revolution he will select next. During late 1992 and early 1993, Mandela's pronouncements became even more chilling. For instance, while on a visit to Beijing in 1992, he stunned Chinese students by saying that the Chinese regime, which had massacred hundreds of students in Tienenmen Square in 1989, was an inspiration "for freedom and democracy." That same year, in an interview with the BBC, he praised the bombings by the Irish Republican Army, saying "civilians must die in the crossfire."

After the death of South African Communist Party leader Chris Hani in April 1993, Mandela was asked on ABC's "Nightline" to mention the leaders he considered the greatest in history. His choices were Abraham Lincoln, Stalin, Lenin, Mao Tse Tung, and Chris Hani! The only surprise is that he did not mention Adolf Hitler in the same breath with Lincoln.

If one adds the names of his other heroes to this list — Arafat, Fidel Castro, Saddam Hussein, Moammar Gadhafi, the regimes in Beijing and Teheran — then one gets a clear picture of a wicked man with wicked heroes who poses a clear danger to South Africa, America, and the West. If he were to head a government, the foreign policy of that government would contribute generously to world terrorism and, perhaps, even war.

It pays for us to understand Nelson Mandela well. He has always been a reckless opportunist, one who would stop at nothing to get power. This is nothing new. In 1945, Lambede, former president of the ANC Youth League, warned about Mandela's opportunism. In 1958, Mandela's former wife and mother of their three small children, learned from newspaper reports that she was being divorced because Mandela had found a young and attractive new love — Winnie. Mandela abandoned his family for Winnie. Thirty years later, Winnie did to Mandela what he had done to his former wife. She abandoned what was then a feeble old man and ran off with a lawyer — young enough to be her son.

According to the traditions of the various black South African ethnic groups, Mandela, at 75, should be a highly respected elder statesman. He is the one who should be sought out by younger leaders for his wise counsel and time-tested wisdom. Instead, he is despised, scorned, and publicly humiliated even by the youth of the organization he leads. To the black South African intelligentsia, he is a laughing stock.

Mandela, the Father of Terrorism in South Africa, has done more harm to the course of black liberation in that troubled land than any other person in living memory. There is no greater shame in South Africa than the fact that Mandela's name is associated with what was once the pride of Africa — the African National Congress.

Chapter 4

Celebrity Churchmen

Great efforts have been made to cover up the "hollow" and "rotten" side of the Church which pretended to fight injustice in the name of the gospel, when in fact, it was worshipping and continues to worship a false god — communism — clothed in the garments of "liberation theology." Karl Marx referred to religion as opium. Cocaine and liberation theology come from the same region of the world, Latin America. Liberation theology has been effectively twisted by the communists to dull the senses of the unsuspecting.

In South Africa, the South African Council of Churches (SACC), Allan Boesak, and Desmond Tutu are among the leading religious representatives of the African National Congress. They, in turn, are worshipped by liberals throughout the world. The SACC is, of course, not a Church, but a political organization with a deceptive religious title. If the ANC prayed, the SACC would be described as the ANC at prayer. It does not. The purpose of the SACC is to confer religious respectability on the communists so that Western liberals can fund communism in South Africa under the guise of supporting churches.

The SACC has negligible support within South Africa. Ninety-nine percent of its budget is covered by funds from the international liberal establishment, especially the United States, Canada, Western Europe, Australia, and New Zealand. If churches in South Africa had any regard for the SACC, they would sacrifice to support the organization financially. The SACC has a long history of mismanagement, corruption, and support for terrorism in South Africa, but the international media requires no accounting for moneys donated to the SACC. Thus, its general secretary, Frank Chikane, a Venda who was defrocked by his own Pentecostal Movement, was able to build himself a half-million-dollar house in Soweto with funds raised in the name of the poor and destitute.

The South African Council of Churches revealed its true colors in 1985 when it became the driving force behind the Kairos Document which called on Christians to join the revolution. The year 1985 was explosive for South Africa. It was the same year the South African Communist Party took over the leadership of the African National Congress. Violence reached new heights that year. South Africa needed cool heads and moral guidance. Instead the SACC added fuel to the fire, by supporting violence.

By using "God sides with the oppressed" as a slogan, the SACC encouraged young people to join violent revolutionary activities resulting in thousands of deaths among blacks and the destruction of property worth billions of dollars. By far the worst crime of the SACC was contributing to the moral death of the young. Short of divine intervention, the young blacks who were morally abused by the SACC will never make it in life. They have nothing on which to build.

Many cunning liberals inside and outside South Africa think they can confuse the unsuspecting by claiming there are two separate groups within the ANC: communists and moderates. This is a bad joke. There are as many moderate leaders within the ANC as there are nuns in a brothel.

Allan Boesak

Allan Boesak, one of the leading black religious spokespersons for the ANC, is a recent convert to communism. This black minister was selected by the international establishment to be a spokesperson for all oppressed black South Africans. His rise to international celebrity status was rapid, thanks to a skillful liberal media campaign. He was given easy access to the powerful of the Western world: kings and queens, lords and ladies, presidents and prime ministers. He was touted as a possible first black prime minister of South Africa. In preparation, he was made president of the World Alliance of Reformed Churches, he was showered with honorary doctorates and the usual liberal-sponsored and politically motivated prizes. With all this favoritism, Boesak still failed to make it. His idea of liberation was having affairs with white women. *Facts on File* (Novmber 14, 1991) reported: "In 1990, following the revelation of an extramarital affair, Boesak quit as minister of a Cape Town church and as president of the World Council of Churches (sic)."

Finally, this darling of the liberals abandoned his wife and children to marry a white television celebrity. He engineered his own downfall and shattered the dreams of his liberal handlers. Disgraced, he was forced to resign from the congregation he led, as well as from the presidency of the World Alliance of Reformed Churches.

Once the liberals turned their back on him, he found himself out in the cold. His only refuge was the ANC. Now Boesak preaches the nationalization of mines and banks, support for the "armed struggle" (burning innocent people to death), and Stalin as one of history's great men.

The Outrageous Archbishop

Anglican Archbishop Desmond Tutu's political role warrants particular scrutiny, especially in light of his call and ongoing support for economic sanctions, which have ruined the lives of millions of black South Africans. Even the Anglican Church in South Africa, which Tutu heads, is deeply divided on the issue of sanctions. Clearly, he does not speak on behalf of his church. In fact, thousands have left the church because of Tutu's sanctions campaign.

His opportunism and ambition are deeply distressing to many. For example, in the 1970s, when the Rev. Leon Sullivan of Philadelphia came up with a set of principles to govern the operations of American corporations in South Africa, Tutu drew up a similar set of his own. When white South African liberals started their journeys to Lusaka to consult with the ANC, Tutu soon made the pilgrimage, too. When the issue of sanctions against South Africa became an internationally popular one, he boarded the bandwagon. He has formed several organizations and named them after himself: the Bishop Tutu Fund for South African Refugees; Tutu Foundation for Development and Relief in Southern Africa; and the Bishop Tutu Fund for Refugees.

He is also quite inconsistent in his support of sanctions. In 1988 he refused to give the commencement address at Tulane University because he said the university held stock in companies doing business in South Africa. He gave the commencement address at Emory University in Georgia, however, even though Emory's dealings with corporations are no different from Tulane's.

He calls for sanctions, yet welcomes monies for his organizations from German and American corporations doing business in South Africa. He accepts substantial financial contributions from Coca-Cola, even though Coca-Cola has rightly refused to withdraw from South Africa. No true leader in the African or any other tradition would dare act in such a manner. These actions are calculated efforts to promote himself and to live up to his celebrity status, which is purely a creation of the Western liberal media.

Tutu's actions are seldom consistent with his words. In 1986, he said the West can "go to hell" (Knight-Ridder, July 1986). Later in the same year he said: "What I know is that if Russians were to come to South Africa today, then most blacks who reject Communism would welcome them as saviors." The millions of dollars Tutu raises annually allegedly to benefit black South Africans are raised in the same West he says can "go to hell." Most of the money goes to what South African blacks refer to as "the Tutu family Trusts," because it benefits Tutu and his family members and friends. No other Anglican bishop in the entire world spends as much time in the U.S. and Europe on matters unrelated to the church as does Archbishop Tutu. In 1989 he even flew to the U.S. just to attend a television show honoring Harry Belafonte!

His claim that he is a socialist ("I find capitalism quite horrendous and unacceptable. I am a socialist." August 10, 1983, *The Canvass*) makes him South Africa's Little Red Bishop and confuses many who know his lifestyle. The socialist bishop lives in Cape Town and also maintains a mansion in Soweto, which was built with money from the World Council of Churches. This money was intended for the poor.

Tutu Comes to America

His appetite for grandeur has now created The Desmond Tutu Center in Atlanta. Perhaps this is to compete with the King Center and the Carter Center. To become a patron of the Tutu Center, one has to fork out $5,000.

In May 1989, Tutu was brought to Washington by his American counterpart, Randall Robinson. The goal, supported by the Congressional Black Caucus, was to lobby for more sanctions against South Africa. If ever anyone needed evidence that neither Tutu nor his American sponsors represent the views of black South Africans, the fiasco in Washington provided it. While Robinson and the other self-appointed "saviors" of black South Africans pushed for more sanctions, Tutu called for "targeted sanctions" and thereby rejected the "mandatory, comprehensive sanctions" which he was sent to advocate. His actions insured that sanctions would not hurt him or the special interests he represents.

Besides the obvious disarray within the ranks of the "saviors," Tutu revealed appalling ignorance when he suggested that the U.S. target transportation, oil, coal, and gold. The 1986 Anti-Apartheid Act cut off transportation links between the

U.S. and South Africa by denying South Africans carriers landing rights at U.S. airports. Oil is already covered by the 1977 UN embargo, and coal by the Act passed by the U.S. Congress in 1986. Finally, the call for sanctions against South African gold revealed economic illiteracy. The world monetary system relies on gold, 60 percent of which in the West comes from South Africa. There will always be a market for South African gold and it is a dangerous illusion to think that sanctions against gold will ever work well enough to put economic pressure on South Africa.

Tutu continues the wanton destruction of his country and, the unnecessary suffering of his people, because he profits from the exercise. He takes his instructions from the ANC and the international liberal establishment, not from his Church, his people, or his conscience.

In light of the demonstrated suffering which blacks endure as a result of sanctions and disinvestment, Tutu's support of sanctions can only be described as cynical, cruel, irresponsible, and phony. If wanton suffering is such a good and necessary price for freedom, then Tutu and others like him should dispose of their considerable wealth and suffer with the poor: the millions of squatters at Cross Roads and Kayelitsha near Cape Town, those in Soweto near Johannesburg, and Kwamashu in Durban. An Anglican layman in Pretoria, who knows Tutu well, describes him as "spiritually empty" and "the most corrupt Archbishop the Anglican Church in South Africa has ever had."

Winning the Nobel Prize

In 1984, Archbishop Tutu won the Nobel Peace Prize. The choice certainly was not based on demonstrated peace work within South Africa or anywhere else in the world. Another South African, Chief Albert Lutuli, won the prize in 1961. He was a statesman of enormous stature who led the original ANC peacefully during its most difficult times. He built lasting bridges among the various South African racial groups. He sought no personal gain or promotion. He never even sought to be president of the ANC. He was, in the tradition of black ethnic groups in South Africa, asked by others to lead. He carried himself with simple humility. The 1984 prize would have more legitimately been awarded to Chief Mangosuthu Buthelezi, or the late Alan Paton, or the late Bishop Alphaeus Zulu. Instead it was awarded to Archbishop Desmond Tutu who has said "Look, I support the ANC, I support them to the hilt" (*Sunday Times*, December 29, 1985). (Ironically, the ANC despises him but sees him as a useful tool.)

Because he has aligned himself with the ANC and is, in fact, their chief religious spokesman, he has highly politicized the Anglican Church in South Africa. As a result, the church is so divided over the issues of sanctions and armed struggle that the courageous voices of such powerful church leaders as Archbishop Joost de Blank, Bishop Reeves, Bishop Colin Winter, and the Rev. Michael Scott, among others, are muted and garbled beyond recognition.

Those who once hoped that a black man at the head of the Anglican Church in South Africa would shorten the days of their misery have watched in disbelief as Tutu, while prospering, has supported actions, such as sanctions and the armed struggle, which can only drive blacks into a bottomless quagmire of destruction, despair, and death. How can Tutu call for sanctions when they have caused 50 percent unemployment nationwide?

Tutu's support for the "revolution" has made the Anglican Church irrelevant in South Africa. In the black-on-black violence which has claimed thousands of lives and left behind thousands of orphans, the once-respected Anglican Church is powerless. The Anglican Church cannot be a reconciling force among the rival black groups. Sadly, the politicized church cannot be a peacemaker. Tutu has made the Church part of the problem.

Why then, was he awarded a prize for peace? It was awarded at the urging of the ANC, which has the full backing of the Scandinavian countries, including Norway. His selection discredits the honor which has stood for so much in the past.

Tutu's vanity and opportunism know no bounds. This supporter of the barbaric ANC/SACP alliance, which has committed unspeakable atrocities against defenseless, poor, black South Africans, has yet another "Tutu" organization in Cape Town, the Tutu Center for Reconciliation and Peace. The word *tutu* means shrub which bears black shiny berries and whose seeds are very poisonous. The Archbishop has certainly sown his fair share of poisonous seeds inside South Africa and around the world. What he means by "reconciliation" is handing over all power to the violent, communist-led ANC.

Normally one would have expected the Archbishop to condemn in no uncertain terms the barbarism of the ANC. This organization has urged the youth to set up street committees to intimidate township residents and "people's courts." In these courts, young children sit in judgment of adults and sentence them to public flogging and death by burning. The same young children are known as "comrades" or "young lions" and will organize the gang-rape of their own mothers unless these women support the ANC. Tutu is silent.

Once Tutu threatened to leave South Africa and go into exile if the violence did not end. The ANC escalated the violence and the Archbishop is still in South Africa. He only leaves to make media events or to preach the communist gospel abroad.

When will the Archbishop demand that the remains of young, black South Africans, who were murdered by the ANC, be brought back from the jungles of Angola, Tanzania, Uganda, and Zambia for proper burial in their places of birth? The Nobel Laureate's voice is conspicuous by its silence in the face of barbarism and evil. Only when the communists are on the receiving end of pain does the bishop wake from his slumber and attack the government, the Inkatha Freedom Party, or the so-called "Third Force."

Tutu the Apostate

In April of 1993, Christians around the world watched the televised funeral of slain Communist Party General Secretary Chris Hani in disbelief. Not only did Tutu lead other cassock-clad clergy in the toi-toi, the communist-revolutionary-frenzy-inspiring dance, but he preached the sermon at the funeral of a communist. Imagine the international media outcry if the Pope were to dance and preach at the funeral of the Italian Communist Party chief or if Billy Graham were to dance and preach at the funeral of Gus Hall, the American Communist Party chief. Again, the media has a separate, preordained standard for what is acceptable in South Africa.

Neither the South African Council of Churches, nor Allan Boesak, nor Desmond Tutu represent the Christian communities in South Africa. They don't represent the poor who aspire to peace and freedom, either. They are tools of the Western liberal establishment. Once this establishment has used them to its satisfaction, they will be dropped and shunned like the plague.

Chapter 5

The Anti-Apartheid Business International

Moral Pressure

After capital began to leave South Africa following the Sharpeville massacre in March 1960, the hated pass laws were suspended. This led the original ANC to place great faith in the power of international moral pressure. The decision to launch an international political campaign against South Africa was intended to persuade the international community to use this power to end apartheid peacefully. The aim was to have the so-called international community wage psychological warfare against the authorities in Pretoria. Some countries had already shown considerable interest in what was going on in South Africa.

As early as 1946, India had complained to the United Nations (UN) about the treatment of people of Indian descent in South Africa. At that time only three African countries, Egypt, Ethiopia, and Liberia were members of the UN. In 1952 the UN passed its first resolution against apartheid. Beginning with 1957, when Ghana became independent, African representation in the UN grew rapidly, particularly between 1960 and 1975.

The UN is supposedly governed by its Charter, regardless of membership composition. Article 2 (7) of the Charter forbids the world body from intervening "in matters which are essentially within the domestic jurisdiction of any state" and does not require members "to submit such matters to settlement under the present Charter." Section VI of the Charter recommends what member states can do if another member does not behave according to international standards — whatever those may be.

Section VII of the Charter mandates the UN to "take action against a member state if the actions of such a member constitute a threat to international peace and security, a breach of internal peace and security, or an act of aggression." Under Section VII the UN is authorized to impose "comprehensive mandatory" sanctions and to police their strict implementation.

Recently, for example, the Iraqi invasion and occupation of Kuwait, a sovereign state, was considered by the UN to warrant invoking Section VII. Nelson Mandela has stated publicly that the UN sanctions against Iraq were motivated by racism, not its Charter. According to him, action was taken against Iraq because Iraqis are "brown-skinned." Neither Mandela nor the press seemed to find a trace of irony in this.

When the original ANC took the case of apartheid to the UN in the early 1960s, it was aware of the provisions of the UN Charter, regarding "domestic jurisdiction" and exceptions. It nevertheless approached the UN in the hope that the UN's sustained moral disapprobation of apartheid would eventually have an impact on its proponents.

From a practical standpoint, it was a good time to go to the UN for moral support. The walls of colonialism were crumbling all over Africa and it appeared that the world would see the clear contradiction in supporting decolonization while supporting apartheid. By going to the UN and asking for nonviolent action against South Africa, the original ANC was clearly distancing itself from the pro-violence South African Communist Party.

International Law

At the UN, the moral approach was quickly forgotten and a legal/political battle ensued. As black countries became independent, they joined the UN in increasing numbers. They forged alliances with other former colonial and oppressed peoples from Asia, South America, and the Caribbean. They received much support from the communist block of nations and many western nations who felt guilty about Europe's colonial past. The newly independent African nations came to the UN riding on a tide of self-righteousness. They were the aggrieved parties. They had been brutalized and exploited by western imperialists. They were blameless and opposed to all forms of racism including apartheid. They stood for democracy and human dignity. Africa condemned apartheid in the harshest possible terms. It was called "inhuman" by Guinea, "slavery" by Nigeria, "a cancer" by Algeria, and "a catalyst of violence" by Tanganyika, now Tanzania.

Many Western countries agreed that the UN should invoke Section VI of the Charter because this only amounted to recommending what member states could do. In 1962, the Africans, inexperienced in international law, were able nonetheless to get a resolution through the UN Security Council calling on the UN to impose comprehensive mandatory sanctions against South Africa in accordance with Section VII of its Charter. The U.S. vetoed the measure calling it "inappropriate" and "ineffective." Britain and France concurred. These three countries which have veto power in the Security Council have maintained this position since 1962, but only when dealing with apartheid South Africa.

African members of the UN tried to bypass the Security Council. Since 1966, they and their backers have forced the UN to hold conferences on apartheid in various parts of the world, including Zambia, Oslo, Paris, Havana, Lagos, Geneva, London, and Vienna. Scores of regional conferences in every conceivable part of the world were also held. Although millions of dollars were spent on them, all they did was pass an ever-increasing and a meaningless number of toothless anti-apartheid resolutions.

In 1963, African members of the UN got the Security Council to pass a resolution which called on member states to refrain from selling arms, ammunition, and military vehicles to South Africa. After the resolution was passed, western nations, including the U.S. went to great lengths to explain that the resolution was a mere recommendation and, therefore, not binding.

In 1977, I was part of a team which lobbied extensively at the UN for an arms embargo against South Africa. This followed the shooting to death in 1976 of almost a thousand black school children, most of them in Soweto, who were demonstrating against an inferior system of education. The international reaction to this wanton killing convinced us that the civilized world would not want to arm South Africa any longer. We were successful. The UN imposed a mandatory arms embargo against South Africa.

After the vote, we were jubilant. Many delegates from around the world congratulated us and assured us that the UN was fully behind the blacks in South Africa. Yet today, more than a decade later, South Africa is not only self-sufficient in military hardware, but actually exports arms, ammunition, and military vehicles to some of her harshest critics and to some of the very countries that voted for the embargo in 1977. In South Africa a mandatory embargo — stronger than targeted (limited) sanctions — produced self-sufficiency and profit, not capitulation.

In the same year, the UN called for an oil embargo against South Africa. Yet oil continued to flow in abundance to South Africa, despite the fact that all the oil-producing and exporting countries are members of the UN. In fact, today, South Africa boasts the largest oil reserves on the continent, excluding oil-producing countries.

1977 also heard the UN Security Council call on countries with nuclear technology not to share it with South Africa. Yet a 1980 study by the UN concluded that South Africa had acquired all the technology needed to manufacture nuclear weapons and their delivery systems. The same UN member states which voted for an arms embargo against South Africa helped South Africa to develop weapons of mass destruction, including nuclear weapons.

In 1993, President de Klerk revealed that South Africa had actually produced six nuclear weapons during the embargo period. There are many who believe that the admission was designed to conceal a much more extensive weapons program. Suffice it to say it would be folly to take de Klerk's word at face value.

UN Hypocrisy

UN members, on the question of South Africa, have consistently acted against their own resolutions. Future historians will be hard-pressed to find worse forms of international hypocrisy than the UN's call for sanctions against South Africa.

At the UN, the fight against apartheid has traditionally been spearheaded by the African states. They have usually been supported by many Asian, Latin American, and Scandinavian countries, as well as the former Soviet block of nations. When African nations first joined the UN in significant numbers in the early 1960s, they were emerging from colonial domination. They were just beginning to govern their own countries and their leaders had not yet committed the serious crimes against their own people which would come to typify their rule. Much of the West was feeling guilty about its colonial past. Too little was known about the goings-on behind the iron curtain. The Africans had a powerful moral voice.

This, however, did not last very long. South Africa was able to gain time by arguing what was difficult to dispute, namely, that apartheid was an internal matter. The strategy worked. Soon the Africans discovered that democracy is not a joy-ride. Ethnic and tribal wars began in "free" African states accompanied by undemocratic measures such as the abolition of opposition parties, suspension of constitutional rule, military dictatorships, economic decline, corruption, incompetence, and wars. The moral voice at the UN became weaker. Today it is nonexistent. South Africa was clearly not the sole custodian of tyranny, nor was South African tyranny the worst. Apartheid was said to be unique only in that it was legalized racial tyranny.

If African nations emerging from colonialism had allowed the seeds of democracy to take root in their newly independent countries; if the different ethnic groups and tribes had been able to co-exist peacefully; if they had been able to build their economies; if they had respected the rule of law and the constitutions they had accepted, then their moral voice at the UN and in other international forums would still carry enormous weight. Such examples would have assured the whites in South Africa that progress, prosperity, and peace are possible in a multi-racial democracy. The brutal tyrannies of African rulers is the overriding factor in the UN's dismal failure to have a positive impact on South Africa. By oppressing and terrorizing their own people, these regimes, despite their rhetoric, proved to white South Africans the danger of what the UN was promoting in the country.

The UN continued to pass resolutions against South Africa with predictable regularity. Today there are hundreds of UN resolutions in place, none of which has any practical value. They are damning evidence of African foolishness and world hypocrisy.

The impotence of the UN on South Africa gradually led to independent anti-apartheid actions all over the world. Citizens of various countries, especially Europeans, boycotted South African goods. In some countries, dock workers refused to load or off-load South African ships. In the U.S., middle- and upper-middle-class white students at Ivy League universities demonstrated on their campuses against apartheid.

Private Sanctions

What started as sporadic actions by citizens who felt morally and ethically bound to oppose apartheid, gradually developed into institutions. In the mid-1970s, anti-apartheid organizations which operated as nonprofit entities began to appear. In time, an international Anti-Apartheid Movement (AAM) developed into a multi-billion dollar industry with its own bureaucracy and agenda. This agenda had two prongs: (1) to coerce individuals and institutions like churches and universities into divesting themselves of shares in corporations that do business in South Africa, and, (2) to force governments to impose economic sanctions against South Africa.

The UN is not an international moral-supreme court. It is a political stock exchange where votes are traded. There are no principles involved. During my tenure at the UN, from 1975 to 1980, African votes were sold for as little as five U.S. dollars apiece! That was during the cold war when East and West were competing for Third World votes.

African governments were driven by self-interest, greed, hypocrisy, and stupidity. They called for sanctions by day and did business with South Africa by night.

Australia supported sanctions against South Africa to express its opposition to apartheid. Yet, Australia treats its black indigenous population, the Aborigines, more inhumanely than blacks are treated in South Africa. When whites first arrived in Australia, there were over 300,000 Aborigines. Today, they number less than half that and are dying out fast. Racism and genocide in Australia surpass anything South Africa has ever experienced, but you won't see headlines about it. Australia points a finger at South Africa in a desperate effort to divert international attention away from its own abhorrent racism.

There is another sinister motive on Australia's part. South Africa was outselling Australia in coal and uranium. In order to capture these important markets, Australia supported sanctions against South Africa. While calling for sanctions, both

Australia and New Zealand bought South African gold to mint their coins, earning them astronomical profits.

Canada is another case in point. The Mohawk Indians, whose land was stolen from them by the Canadians in the first place, are victims of vicious racism in Canada. How can a country which blatantly practices racism at home condemn racism in another country? Even the Canadian white tribes — the French-speaking and the English-speaking — are at each other's throats. They cannot solve their own problems, yet they meddle in South Africa's domestic affairs. Like Australia, Canada seeks to divert attention from its own racism and to capture the gold coin market which, until sanctions were imposed against the Krugerrand, was controlled by South Africa.

American Duplicity

Nowhere in the world was the call for sanctions against South Africa louder than in the American. It has become a major preoccupation of the black leadership and the white liberal establishment. Even in 1993 the call for sanctions against South Africa is still being heard in America. A closer examination of anti-South African activity, however, reveals that the battle which is being waged actually has little or nothing to do with South Africa. This is an internal American battle, designed to divert attention from America's own racial problems, which is being fought on South African turf. These different and differing American forces argue that if the South African economy is destroyed, the Afrikaners will capitulate and democracy will descend on South Africa overnight. The latest demand is that sanctions not be lifted until an ANC government is in place. Economic, political, and social change will magically emerge out of a devastated economy, thanks to democracy's proven effectiveness.

This kind of reasoning strikes many South Africans as odd. After all, the greatest degree of positive social change in the U.S. took place during the three decades following World War

II when the American economy was at its strongest. A strong economy fueled rapid economic, political, and social change. Unless this is just voodoo logic, why should and how can a devastated economy bring about dramatic change in South Africa? How can a free-market democracy arise from these ashes? The exponents of this abnormal theory never state how long it will take for sanctions to bring about the desired change, nor are they able to spell out how the process will work, particularly given the complexities of international trade and South Africa's possession of strategic minerals. Experience has proven that human greed and self interest will always provide South Africa with adequate customers, as has happened whenever sanctions have been imposed.

A weak economy actually fuels racial strife. When the Germans accepted the racial theories of the Nazis, their economy was weak and millions of Germans were unemployed. The same reaction to hard times is affecting immigrants in Germany today. As the American economy shows signs of strain, racial tension is revealing itself in some of the most unusual places: university and high school campuses. In South Africa, a struggling economy is fostering the same rise in white and black racial tension. The weak economy is also fueling an escalation of inter-ethnic, deadly violence which has already claimed thousands of innocent lives.

The American call for sanctions demonstrates serious hypocrisy. The Americans, almost three decades ago, stated at the UN that sanctions against South Africa were "inappropriate" and "ineffective." That has been the officially stated position of every administration since John Kennedy. In the UN Security Council, the U.S., by the use of its veto, has made sure that comprehensive, mandatory sanctions were not imposed on South Africa. Even President Jimmy Carter, the "Guru of Human Rights," opposed sanctions against South Africa when he was President and had the power to impose them. Now that he is no longer in office, he favors imposing economic sanctions against South Africa!

In the U.S. and other parts of the Western world, ordinary citizens who were appalled by apartheid, sought in various ways, to express their distaste for apartheid either as individuals or through churches, synagogues, and institutions of learning. These people were genuinely concerned for all South Africans. Unfortunately, all good things can be corrupted. So it was with anti-apartheid activity in the U.S. By the end of the 1970s it had become a lucrative industry. Ironically, as had been the case at the UN, where ignorant Africans were in the forefront of the battle for sanctions, in America, ignorant blacks led the fight against the people of South Africa.

Devastating Effects

Sanctions and disinvestment cause job losses. This creates poverty, hunger, disease, homelessness, and death. Unemployment fosters the crime and violence which lead also to senseless death. The end result of sanctions is negative and disastrous. In modern history, sanctions have never been known to achieve the positive results for which they were intended. South Africa is no exception.

The refusal by many international banks to extend new loans to South Africa, or to reschedule the repayment of interest on existing loans, smacks of opportunism and hypocrisy. Many of these banks are all too willing to write off huge amounts owed by black African dictators whose present records on human rights are far worse than South Africa's. The banks are not motivated by morality. If they were, they would use the same yardstick all over Africa and the world.

The loss of overseas markets and the high cost of circumventing sanctions is straining the South African economy. The result is that high school and college graduates cannot find employment and are left idle. South African blacks are a proud and hard-working people, traditionally embarrassed by handouts and welfare. It is a disgrace for an able-bodied person to live as a parasite. If the policy of sanctions is continued, black South Africans will soon form a colossal legion to march at the head of black Africa's existing parade of beggars.

Recent history proves progress is possible in an economically-strong South Africa. The black trade unions in South Africa were legalized at a time when the economy was booming. A strong economy made it possible for workers to negotiate for better wages and working conditions, thereby achieving a higher standard of living for their families. Economic strength and security provided the energy for trade unions to fuel political changes. Trade unions can only suffer with job losses. For every black worker who loses a job, between eight and twelve dependents suffer. Sanctions are anti-worker, not anti-government. To advocate sanctions against South Africa is to discourage change, and support de facto apartheid.

Both poverty and hardship are on the rise in South Africa, in rural areas and cities. Welfare organizations now feed young hungry children, something hitherto unknown in the country. Parents who can find work at a living wage can feed their own children. Death is also taking its toll, particularly among the very young and the aged, who have the least defense against malnutrition and its related diseases.

Despair is causing large-scale violence, especially among young blacks. This is especially true in Natal, Cross Roads (near Cape Town), and Soweto where sanctions deal their most devastating blows. Here, the level of black-on-black violence is unprecedented both in brutality and in the number of innocent victims. The most hideous and barbaric form of violence in the history of South Africa, the ANC's practice of burning political opponents alive in public, is largely a direct result of idleness and despair. This subhuman practice which is carried out in the name of liberation was introduced to South Africa by white and Indian communists. Blacks have no tradition of burning human beings. Europeans and Asians do. The practice is further evidence that blacks in the ANC leadership merely dance to the tune of their white and Indian masters. They are directed to murder their own people.

Because of sanctions and disinvestment, many of the progressive social programs which were started by American corporations in South Africa, have now been canceled for lack of funds. Ironically, these programs were designed to benefit the victims of apartheid and assist them in their struggle to bring about democracy and reconciliation. They included company-sponsored education, housing developments, job training, and loans for purposes of starting small businesses. Black victims of apartheid were being equipped with the most potent weapons against oppression: knowledge, skills, and economic muscle. The withdrawal of American corporations and the subsequent closing of some of these outstanding programs is a major setback to preparing black South Africans for leadership in post-apartheid South Africa. American corporations that have withdrawn from South Africa have been replaced by others from countries which do not necessarily share the same commitment or who cannot afford to finance the social programs to the extent that the American companies did.

America's management style and the fair employment practices which American managers brought to South Africa are slowly being lost. An insulated country like South Africa needs to be exposed to different and constructive ways of doing things. One way of allaying white fears, some of which are legitimate given the performance of black Africa, is to demonstrate that blacks and whites benefit from working with each other. The American corporations provided an environment where this could be done by hiring and promoting blacks.

White South African businessmen have become very wealthy as a result of buying out such departing American giants as Ford Motor Company, General Motors, and Mobil Oil. The corporations were sold at rock-bottom prices when they yielded to pro-sanctions pressure in the U.S. They were not sold to blacks. The consensus in South Africa is that sanctions have made "the rich richer and the poor poorer."

The actual abolition of apartheid within the structure and practices of American corporations in South Africa added credibility when they urged the government to abolish apartheid. That voice is gone. Those committed to working for peaceful change in South Africa feel cheated and abandoned by America.

The negative effects of sanctions are not limited to South Africa. The economies of Botswana, Lesotho, Malawi, Mozambique, Namibia, Swaziland, Zaire, and Zimbabwe are closely linked to that of South Africa. For example, about half the male populations of Botswana and Lesotho are employed in South Africa. The entire southern African region has more than 100 million people. Unless the sanctions madness is stopped, the whole region will be turned into an economic Hiroshima. All hope of democracy will die along with the economy and the damage may never be fully repaired. Ironically, it is the American, European, and Japanese taxpayers who will be expected to foot the bill for the attempted rehabilitation of post-sanction southern Africa.

Since his release, Mandela has spent much of his time globetrotting and begging for money from the very corporations he says must leave South Africa. Regaining the ground lost to sanctions will cost a fortune in human lives and outside money, especially if it is attempted using the ANC brand of communism.

Those who recklessly call for the destruction of the South African economy have cunningly avoided the real issues which are linked to sanctions. While pretending to take the moral high ground, they have never provided the moral justification for employing indiscriminate punitive measures, knowing full well that sanctions are most harmful to those who are already bearing the brunt of apartheid, namely the workers and the poor.

With dogmatic tenacity and blind arrogance, they refuse to accept that even the arms embargo (the equivalent of comprehensive, mandatory sanctions) imposed by the whole world against South Africa in 1977 has failed dismally. I am one of those who worked tirelessly for the embargo. It is now far too late even for the UN to act. The feeble, selective sanctions which have been childishly debated for decades, are an idea whose time has passed — if such a time ever existed at all.

Sanctions foster only economic chaos, anarchy, and social disintegration. Given the disastrous experiences of black independent states, only the enemies of Africa can wish South Africa to join the African club of beggar nations. It is time for those who want a better future for all South Africans to participate actively in a program which will end apartheid and put in its place a system which will be democratic in intent, in application, and in results. South Africa could be the anchor for positive change across all of Africa.

Progress in South Africa has been achieved by South Africans themselves, black and white, not by sanctions. For more than 300 years they have struggled to make their country and nation democratic. They were working at this long before the U.S. Congress or State Department, not to mention the so-called black civil rights leadership, discovered that South Africa exists.

Even though sanctions have had a crippling effect on the South African economy, it is not, as Mandela said on the day of his release "in ruins." The South African economy remains the strongest in Africa and carries on its back the economies of several other African countries. It is not too late.

Thirty years ago when most African countries became independent, there was great hope for the future prosperity of Africa. Ghana, which became independent in 1957, inherited a healthy economy from the British. Today Ghana is an economic ruin. Liberia, which was established by freed American slaves, had a healthy and growing economy until the beginning of the 1980s. Today, as a result of war and corruption, Liberia is an economic ruin. Uganda, which under British rule was "The Pearl Of Africa," is in ruins and ravaged by AIDS.

Again, if the South African economy is destroyed, it will never recover. South Africa may be the last hope for the continent. The sooner normal economic activity is established between South Africa and the rest of the world, the better it will be for all of Africa — and the rest of the world.

Chapter 6

The Black American Mercenaries

Skin color does not define people, nor does it measure what people feel. Otherwise the problems in Northern Ireland would not exist, since all those involved are white. Nor would Arabs and Jews be at each other's throats in the Middle East. Blacks in South Africa would not be slaughtering one another, either.

Against this background it is astounding how the media, in collusion with relatively few black Americans, have successfully created the false impression that black Americans as a group have some special relationship with black South Africans similar to the relationship between American Jews and the Jews in Israel. It is astounding because there are neither historical nor cultural ties between the two peoples. Even if one were to stretch the argument about "similar experiences of oppression" the special relationship would cover all of black Africa. It would at least emphasize those countries in Africa where blacks are infinitely worse off than blacks in South Africa — Somalia, Uganda, Angola, Sudan, Mozambique, Ethiopia, and Liberia, to name but a few. If there were to be any special relationship between black Americans and an African nation it would be with Liberia, which would be similar to the relationship between American Jews and Israelis.

Liberia was founded by freed American slaves over 100 years ago. There are blood ties between Liberians and black Americans. Yet in spite of the ongoing human tragedy in Liberia, black American leaders who cannot sleep at night because of apartheid in South Africa, are unmoved by the wanton slaughter of their own relatives in Liberia. It is a most serious anomaly.

The only relationships that exist between black South Africans and black Americans are personal. They are a result of friendships and business ties between individuals and families, or the ties which have been cemented through marriage. There is also no such thing as black American support for black South Africans. There is instead a large group of black Americans who are staunch supporters of the communist-led ANC.

Randall Robinson

Chief among these is Randall Robinson, the black American authority on how economic devastation is beneficial to black South Africans. He is a relative newcomer to the so-called anti-apartheid scene. In November of 1991, Robinson led a crusade to South Africa and met with the ANC. *Facts on File* (November 14, 1991) gave this account:

> "A delegation of about 30 black Americans ended a three-day visit to South Africa. The African National Congress had invited them to examine the effects of recent government reforms, and they met exclusively with ANC representatives. One traveler, Randall Robinson, head of the U.S. lobby group TransAfrica, accused U.S. President Bush of failing to use his influence to help curb township strife. Rep. Maxine Waters (D.-CA) vowed to press American states and cities to maintain sanctions against South Africa. Other visitors included recording artist Quincy Jones and former tennis champion Arthur Ashe."

He burst into prominence in 1984 when he organized demonstrations outside the South African embassy in Washington. Those who took part were arrested and spent a few hours in police custody. It was a publicity stunt which helped to promote Robinson and his struggling organization *TransAfrica*, which supposedly lobbies for Africa and the Caribbean.

Even though Robinson is quite ignorant about South Africa and the complexities of the situation, his demonstrations won him appearances on "Nightline" and the "Today Show." This exposure enabled him to raise money, not to help the victims of apartheid whose condition he was exploiting, but for himself and his organization. TransAfrica, which started its operation in a one-bedroom apartment, has recently purchased its own headquarters in Washington, D.C. for more than three million dollars. The five-story, 15,000 square foot mansion once housed the German embassy.

Even though this black organization is supposed to lobby on behalf of all of Africa, it focuses almost exclusively on South Africa because apartheid is an emotional issue and a good fundraiser. Robinson and TransAfrica are silent about the atrocities committed by black African tyrants in Burundi, Rwanda, Sudan, Somalia, Chad, Liberia, Uganda, the Central African Republic, Ghana, Nigeria, among others. Such selective criticism is evidence of moral bankruptcy, and black racism.

In 1986, as a result of Robinson's lobbying, the U.S. Congress passed what is euphemistically known as the Comprehensive Anti-apartheid Act of 1986. Since Robinson does not and has never held elective office, it was left to the Congressional Black Caucus to debate the issue in Congress.

Comprehensive Sanctions?

Historically, as in the UN debate, the U.S. has been completely opposed to international, comprehensive, mandatory sanctions against South Africa. Why and how would the U.S. impose the same sanctions on its own? Surely, if the purpose were to put pressure on Pretoria, world pressure would be far more effective than pressure from one country, as was clearly demonstrated when the U.S. went to the UN to declare war on Iraq. If sanctions were going to dismantle apartheid, then world sanctions would do the job faster and more efficiently, but the U.S. opposed world sanctions in the UN!

Comprehensive sanctions would include not just commodities but all forms of communication and diplomatic relations. At any rate, by 1986, the world already knew that the oil and arms embargoes against South Africa had failed dismally. The Black Congressional Caucus initiated and helped pass a piece of hypocritical legislation which had nothing to do with helping the victims of apartheid, but was designed by cunning politicians and TransAfrica to be a vote catcher in an election year.

Though termed comprehensive, the Act actually specified the items which were not to be imported into the U.S. These included agricultural products, coal, uranium, textiles, iron, and steel. South African Airways was barred from landing in the U.S. The white liberal establishment was the largest backer of this legislation. Nothing was done to make sure that the sanctions would be mandatory. As a result, iron and steel, for example, which were on the "comprehensive" list, were freely imported into the U.S. The Black Caucus, though fully aware of this, was silent. The so-called "comprehensive" list was important for what it excluded. South Africa's big money earners were somehow not on the list: gold, diamonds, platinum, chrome, manganese, and vanadium. In the worst days of apartheid, which included 1986, the black mine workers were among those most exploited in South Africa. Not only were they underpaid, they lived away from their families for eleven months in the year, sometimes even several years, and often had to live in overcrowded, squalid, and unhealthy hostels. How significant that the 1986 Act, which the Black Caucus spearheaded, specifically excluded those hit hardest by apartheid by excluding the strategic metals they mined!

The Black Caucus

Given their lack of astuteness, the Black Caucus may not have realized that by spearheading legislation against South Africa they were acting contrary to international law, just as the black African States at the UN were out of step with international law when they called on the UN to impose sanctions against South Africa.

The relevant UN laws exist to prevent international meddling in the affairs of member states. For example, the way America treats its indigenous Indian population is an internal matter. In 1990, Mandela, as part of his grand posturing, promised the American Indians that he would liberate them. They are still waiting.

South Africa is not the 51st state and the people of South Africa have never requested that the U.S. Congress legislate for economic sanctions against them. The action of Congress, in addition to being hypocritical and illegal, is paternalistic in that it decides for the South African people what is good for them. The Act itself is thoroughly evil in that it is indiscriminate in its application. Sanctions have hurt the black victims of apartheid far more than they have the South African government which is responsible for apartheid.

When the Act was being debated in Congress, the American people should also have been told that the exiled, high-living, communist-led ANC in Lusaka, Zambia actually called for the sanctions, not the hard-working black people inside South Africa. The people in Lusaka who were calling for the sanctions had been out of South Africa for thirty years. During that period they had not spent a day earning an honest living. Like Jesse Jackson, they went around the world talking about issues they hardly understood or cared about. They were not the chosen representatives of the South African people. They live on international handouts. In South Africa they are known as the Loafers of Lusaka. Some of them have amassed considerable wealth out of the suffering of their fellow South Africans, the ones they claim to represent.

Why impose sanctions on the Pretoria regime and not on the murderous regime in Ethiopia where millions of blacks were killed by fellow blacks? What about Rwanda, where the Hutu practice real apartheid against the minority Tutsi tribe? And what about Burundi, where the Tutsi have slaughtered hundreds of thousands of Hutus in cold blood? At the time when the Black Caucus was pushing for sanctions against South Africa, more than 20 military regimes in Africa ignored the constitutional rights of citizens, if any even existed. What about the one-party states — Ghana, Liberia, Somalia, Kenya — where citizens could not even vote? What about states like Zaire where the wealth of the nation belongs to the president and the citizens live in abject poverty perpetually? Why is white tyranny unacceptable when even worse black tyranny is protected?

Rancor in the Civil Rights Ranks

The black American leadership of the civil rights movement plays an important part in misleading the American people in general and black Americans in particular about the reality of South Africa. The uninvited meddling of this group in the internal affairs of South Africa stems from its dismal failure to achieve the goals set forth in the original movement under Dr. Martin Luther King, Jr. This movement, which at one time promised to transform American society, died with Dr. King in April 1968, and lies buried with him in Atlanta. Dr. King's disciples (Jesse Jackson, several members of the Black Caucus, Joseph Lowery, his widow Coretta Scott King, Andrew Young, and many others across the U.S.) scattered like the frightened disciples of Jesus after his arrest and crucifixion. Unlike Jesus' disciples, who later regrouped and carried on his work as apostles, King's disciples went their several ways to seek fame and fortune for themselves, demonstrating that they had "overcome."

Like the disciples of Jesus, there arose a dispute as to who would be the greatest among them and wear Dr. King's mantle. Instead of settling on a leader for the sake of the movement and what it promised, they decided to wreck the movement and abandon millions of poor black Americans, leaving them without a sense of direction.

Since Dr. King's death, thousands of black Americans have been elected to public office including many of those who once claimed to be part of the civil rights movement. Their success has been accompanied by an unprecedented decline in the quality of life for at least half the black population. Dr. King fought against injustice, poverty, violence, and crime. Today's list of black ills adds alarming teen pregnancy rates, drugs, AIDS, illiteracy, crime, black-on-black violence, school dropouts, and, most serious, the self-destruction of the black family. Martin Luther King, Jr.'s disciples, if they have any interest at all in these issues, certainly offer no solutions.

Many of Dr. King's former associates have developed a simplistic and rather sheepish approach to these devastating problems. They blame everything on racism and project blacks as helpless victims of the white man. They take no responsibility for their obvious failures. They are unwilling to provide meaningful leadership. The false cry of racism provides them with a cover to hide their relentless pursuit of personal ambition, aggrandizement, and greed.

Racism, to be sure, is a fact of life in America, and those guilty of it include members of all races including blacks and whites. Racism is not the prerogative of one particular race. It manifests itself in every part of the world. Japanese-Americans, for example, were victims of racism during World War II. Today, however, they are making phenomenal strides in every area of American activity. Instead of singing the worn-out racism song, they are working hard and achieving their goals, in spite of racism.

Many immigrants, including black Africans, are registering successes in business, academia, and in many different professions. Many refugees who arrive in the U.S. with no knowledge of English work hard and establish themselves. They do not become perpetual welfare cases. Racism and other hardships evoke in them a spirit of determination and a sense of dignity, not dependence.

It is extremely difficult to understand how racism is responsible for black-on-black violence or the problem of drugs in black neighborhoods, or the high dropout rate from schools or the increasing numbers on welfare and the number of black babies born with the AIDS virus. Even more difficult to understand is what racism has to do with black teenage pregnancies which are increasing at an astronomical rate.

It is obvious that young black boys are not being taught to respect little black girls, some of whom become mothers at the tender ages of eleven, twelve, or thirteen. Black girls are not taught to respect themselves. Young black boys and girls are not being taught responsibility. They are not taught traditional values. They lack role models because those who are supposed to be role models have abandoned them — in search of personal glory and ill-gotten wealth. Too many young black children are on their own. Their chances of making it in life are very slim. What is the black American leadership doing? They are busy supporting the march towards communism in South Africa.

The black establishment "leadership" chooses not to deal with these American crises. The challenge presented by these domestic problems has inspired many celebrity black leaders only to turn away from them and pretend that they can solve South Africa's problems. They cannot. They play at escaping from reality, because reality is too painful. And wagging their fingers at South Africa, diverts attention from their failures at home. How can people who are unable to solve their own problems find workable solutions to complex problems in a distant land? Most black South Africans deeply resent the way the black American celebrity leadership uses their suffering for personal gain.

Mind Your Own Business

Even if sanctions were the right strategy, the actions of these leaders would still be unacceptable. The reasons are cultural. The varied South African cultures have their own procedures for handling disputes. The Zulus, for example, say *eyomndeni ayingenwa*, meaning that one does not intrude into other peoples' disputes unless one has been expressly invited as a mediator. A violation of this long-standing cultural norm is an insult which turns the perpetrator into an enemy. The black American groups have no mandate from the victims of apartheid to act on their behalf. The question which stares them in the face is, "Where are the solutions for your own pressing problems?"

In the late '70s, Jesse Jackson went to South Africa and gave unsolicited advice to black leaders. Many South Africans resented his interference and knew that he had no intention of solving any problems in South Africa. He came only to promote himself. It was well known that he had not succeeded in solving any of the black problems in Chicago, his home town. Further, he is most vocal about apartheid and sanctions, yet gladly accepts handsome contributions from companies doing business in South Africa, even those he publicly criticizes.

In February 1990, when news leaked that Mandela would be released, Jackson rushed to Cape Town in an effort to take credit. De Klerk pre-empted the claim stating publicly that Jackson's presence was "irrelevant." In an effort to get a visa at short notice, Jackson told the South African ambassador to Washington that he favored the lifting of sanctions against South Africa. On his arrival in South Africa he met the leaders of the South African Communist Party, including Walter Sisulu, and announced that sanctions should be maintained. Black South Africans who have not forgotten his interference in their affairs, shunned him. Jackson cut short his visit after he was almost killed in Cape Town. He has never told the American people that he owes his life to the hated white South African police who rescued him. He returned to the U.S. without the title he had so desperately sought: "Liberator of Mandela."

Black American mercenaries are not limited to those who are either politically or racially motivated. Many black

American clergy find it easy to violate the very foundations of their own ethics when they deal with South Africa.

In 1987, a black group was formed in Washington, D.C. called the Coalition for Southern Africa (COSA). It was comprised mainly of clergy people led by a number of bishops from the black denomination, the American Methodist Episcopal (AME) Church. One of these bishops had actually served in South Africa and, therefore, was well aware of the situation there.

The group received $765,000 from a number of well-intentioned American corporations, including Mobil Oil, Control Data, Combustion Engineering, Johnson and Johnson, and Pfizer. The money was intended for training black South Africans to run post-apartheid South Africa. Only three students received a total of $5,000 each for one semester at Morris Brown College, which was founded by the AME Church in Atlanta. By the time the students were ready to register for the second semester, COSA and its money had disappeared. The students were left stranded.

The shameful actions of the AME bishops involved with COSA are in sharp contrast to those of leaders of the same denomination who, in the 1890s, helped the black South African leader Dr. John Dube, first President of the original ANC and friend of Booker T. Washington, in his efforts to raise money for his school. Dube named the school Ohlange Institute, and it is the only educational institution founded by a black person in South Africa. Dube named Ohlange "Institute" after Tuskegee Institute, which was a great inspiration to him, especially because it was a living monument to black self-worth. He also wanted to show his special indebtedness to Booker T. Washington.

Black Americans the stature of Booker T. Washington have now been replaced by charlatans like those in TransAfrica.

Mandela in the Big Apple

In June 1991, TransAfrica and others brought Nelson Mandela to the U.S. for a 14-day tour. The road show was impressive. Mandela, the Father of Terrorism in South Africa, was treated like a god wherever he went. Indeed, the black mayor of New York, David Dinkins, ignored the needs of millions of destitute New Yorkers and put the city deeper into debt by organizing a ticker tape parade in honor of Mandela. Dinkins crowned Mandela "the New Moses." I was spared a heart attack by remembering that Moses never reached the Promised Land. Throngs of black Americans turned out to have a glimpse of a hero created by the media *ex nihilo* — out of nothing. The sight of it all was astounding: politicians, clergymen, academics, athletes, artists, journalists, workers, the homeless, business leaders, Christians, Muslims, Jews, atheists all feted a violent communist, even as they mouthed nonviolence. They gave and promised to give tens of millions of dollars without knowing who they were giving it to or why. It was a personal triumph for Randall Robinson, who marketed Mandela and made himself a fortune.

Only Robinson knows what happened to the money raised mainly from hard-working black Americans. The money was supposed to help suffering black South Africans in their fight against apartheid. As of this writing, three years have passed and the money has still not reached South Africa.

Randall Robinson and TransAfrica are attempting to dictate the terms under which American corporations may reinvest in South Africa. Randall Robinson and TransAfrica also want to be the brokers between black business people in South Africa and American businesses.

Before signing Robinson on as middleman, American business must ask whether Randall Robinson or TransAfrica has any authority to handle anything that has to do with South Africa. Robinson, TransAfrica, the Black Caucus, the so-called civil rights leaders, and some black academics form a relatively small band of arrogant black Americans who believe they have a God-given right to meddle, for profit, in the affairs of Africans. Randall Robinson's condescending and paternalistic behavior towards Africa in general is the equivalent of racism. Blacks in South Africa will soon be part of the new government. At that point, TransAfrica's lucrative business of exploiting the suffering of black South Africans will come to an abrupt end.

Black Academia Speaks

Also astounding is the attitude of the many black academics towards South Africa. Objectivity and scholarly integrity disappear from the trained minds of many black academics when they discuss South Africa. Their blind emotional support for Mandela and the rest of the communist band in South Africa proves that many of the black academics who parade as Africa experts are anything but. To speak of an "Africa expert" is, of course, ridiculous. No such thing exists. Africa is a vast and diverse continent more than three times the size of the United States. African peoples speak thousands of different indigenous languages and dialects and represent indigenous cultures, customs, traditions, and histories. African traditional religions differ not just from nation to nation, but from ethnic group to ethnic group, tribe to tribe, and clan to clan within nations. No human being can be an expert on Africa. One might become an expert on the Kikuyu or the Shona or the Baca or the Ashante. But one cannot be an expert on Nigeria or Sudan or South Africa. In South Africa, the Afrikaners are not the Vendas, the Sotho are not the Xhosa, and the Hindu are not Zulus.

Too many of the black American academics offering theories on Africa do not understand her. Richard Joseph, a black American professor of political science at Emory University and the Carter Center's "expert on Africa," is an avid supporter of the communist-led ANC. He condemns Inkatha as an insignificant movement. He has joined other scholars who conduct their research in *New York Times*. Theirs is not scholarship. They quote partisan propaganda. Small wonder black university students are so confused about Africa. They think of Africa as one country. They think all black Africans are culturally the same.

Supporting Violence

Another perplexing behavior of the civil rights leadership is seldom mentioned: their support for violence in South Africa, while they pose as disciples of nonviolence everywhere else.

Coretta Scott King and her Martin Luther King, Jr. Center for Nonviolent Social Change in Atlanta has led the way. Since her husband's murder, Coretta Scott King has claimed to champion the aborted course of her late husband. What evidence can be cited to support that claim? What social change has the Center fostered? Atlanta, where the Center is based, is often rated the leading crime city in the U.S. The Center has no graduates who are skilled in conflict resolution or the methods of nonviolence. No such people have been trained. The Center's chief product is aggrandizement for Coretta Scott King. It attracts money and generates only expenses. It is, in fact, a disservice to the community it is intended to serve. Consider the following:

In January 1992, Winnie Mandela, the notorious wife of Nelson Mandela, was invited by the King Center to lead the annual parade honoring Dr. King in Atlanta. To her credit, Winnie Mandela has never pretended to be a disciple of nonviolence. She may just be the world's most violent woman.

When I asked a black American leader how he could support Winnie, his response was: "I don't care about Winnie's alleged crimes. As long as she is fighting to drive whites into the sea, I will support her." Unfortunately, this is the view of far too many black Americans.

A picture of Winnie Mandela giving the communist salute adorns the entrance to the Martin Luther King, Jr. Center for Nonviolent Change. What hypocrisy! What a travesty! Mrs.

King, who would have us believe that she is devastated by the plight of black South Africans who are ten thousand miles away, seems unmoved by the people living in slum conditions surrounding the plush King Center. The neighborhood is a living reminder that the dream died with Dr. King in Memphis. John Kennedy, Robert Kennedy, and Malcolm X, like Dr. Martin Luther King, Jr., were murdered and left behind widows and children. Only Coretta Scott King has turned the murder of her husband into a money-making spectacle.

The vast majority of black Americans do not act as mercenaries or charlatans when it comes to the issue of South Africa. Some genuinely care. Those who do so are relatively few, because the liberal American media insure that Americans will never get a clear picture of what is going on in South Africa. Were the media to educate readers, listeners, and viewers about the realities of South Africa, the vast majority of Americans, black and white, would reject the ANC with contempt. The media know that Mandela is a buffoon, yet they sell him as a leader just as they have sold the black American mercenaries. Black Americans have made and continue to make outstanding contributions in fields of science, technology, literature, business, and education. This is nothing new. Although they usually go unrecognized, black American women are the backbone of black advancement.

My wife's great-great-grandmother, the famous Ellen Craft, was a slave in Georgia. She masterminded her escape and that of her husband, William. They eventually fled to England. After the Emancipation Proclamation, they returned to South Carolina, where Ellen established a school at Hickory Hill. She taught plantation children by day and adults by night. She was so successful that the Ku Klux Klan burned down the school. Instead of moaning and groaning about racism, the Crafts moved to Savannah, Georgia, where they built another school. They knew the power of education.

Recently, I attended an event in Columbia, South Carolina where twelve black men and women from that state were honored for their outstanding contributions to South Carolina. The honorees included my father-in-law, Herbert DeCosta who, like his father and grandfather, made enormous contributions to the architecture of the city of Charleston. The national media were not there. The same media is always present when Jesse Jackson repeats his nursery rhymes or when he mouths such empty slogans as "keep hope alive." It is clear that the objective of the liberal media is to portray blacks as totally hopeless and helpless beings who cannot survive without the kindness of liberals.

Unfortunately, too many black males have accepted this unrealistic stereotype. As things stand now, the burden of saving black America is squarely on the shoulders of black women. If they fail, it will only be a matter of time before the black race in America is history. The black male celebrity leaders will continue to meddle in South African affairs as long as it is profitable to do so.

The South African situation is treacherously complex, even for South Africans. No one knows what the outcome will be, but one thing is certain. The majority of South Africans will NEVER allow the communists to govern them, no matter how vocally black Americans support the communist-led ANC. The ANC is not even a black-led organization — it is led by whites and Indians — black American support for the communists betrays their ignorance.

Only the South Africans themselves can and will solve South Africa's problems. By the same token, only Americans can solve their own problems. Mutual acceptance of this basic principle can lead to better understanding between the two countries and eventually to genuine cooperation and friendship. Blacks in both countries would benefit.

Chapter 7

The Curse of Modern Liberalism

Liberalism once stood for a political and economic order based on equality, freedom, and opportunity. The early liberals believed in the right of a citizen to rebel against tyrannical governments. This kind of liberalism inspired the English, American, and French revolutions. This lead to the establishment of constitutional governments — meaning government based on the consent of the governed — and the birth of the bill of rights. These early liberals espoused maximum individual freedom and minimum government; capitalism or free enterprise economics.

In the West a significant change occurred in the meaning of liberalism in the 1900s, especially regarding government. Today, liberals believe in massive government interventions including antipoverty measures, civil rights legislation, sexual issues, abortion, and a host of social programs. Perhaps the biggest transformation is that those who still hold the original liberal economic and political views are usually described now as conservative or reactionary. The term "liberal" is clothed in heavy garments of confusion and defies precise definition. Loosely speaking, liberals in our day are those who see government as some economic and political god; the solver of all human problems. If only the government would spend enough money, all human misery would end and everyone would live happily ever after.

Liberalism in South Africa is confusing too, but for different reasons. A great divergence of political views exists among black South Africans, ranging from traditionalists to communists. On one issue, however, there is almost universal agreement among them: they do not trust liberals. The roots of this distrust run deep, going back to the colonialism of the early 18th century. In those days, according to South African terminology, the Afrikaners were considered the conservatives and the white English-speaking colonialists were considered the liberals. Today, of course, the lines are not that clear. When black South Africans speak of liberals, they mean wishy-washy whites.

Liberals and Apartheid

I remember my grandfather, a man of tremendous wisdom. Though he had never seen the inside of a school, he knew Zulu oral history as though he had done a doctorate in the subject. The things he taught us could not be found in any history book, since all early South African history was written by white colonialists and biased, to say the least.

He would say to us: "When dealing with liberals, be vigilant. They will smile at you, and as soon as you turn your back, they will stab you. You can always trust a Boer (Afrikaner). If he says he hates you, he means it. If he says he likes you, he means that too." For him, liberals were treacherous people.

These were not just the views of one old man. Black South Africans have mountains of stories about liberal treachery. One of the most famous is about how the liberals arrived in South Africa with their Bibles. At that time blacks had land but no Bibles. The liberals gave blacks Bibles and told them to close their eyes and pray. When the blacks opened their eyes, the liberals had the land and the blacks were left holding Bibles.

It is true that the Afrikaner introduced apartheid in South Africa. But black people faired no better under British rule. Since 1948, when apartheid was introduced in South Africa, the

National Party has won every all-white election with majorities which clearly showed that a substantial body of liberals were voting for apartheid while condemning the system verbally. After all, apartheid showered copious favors on all white South Africans. While liberals shed oceans of crocodile tears over the evils of apartheid, they simultaneously feasted on the sumptuous apartheid meal. While they criticized the government, they amassed wealth by exploiting black workers. Liberals never hesitated to send their children to the best segregated schools, use segregated hospitals and even segregated churches. The liberal, English-speaking churches owned and operated segregated schools and hospitals. While the liberals made a great deal of empty noise in the all-white parliament, no demonstrable difference existed between them and the apartheid regime. Liberals in South Africa have never practiced true liberalism, otherwise they would have taken steps to overthrow the tyrannical apartheid government. Instead they have always been willing bedfellows.

Liberals own most of the media in South Africa. True to their incorrigibly opportunistic practices, they now back the communist-led ANC, because whites and Indians run it. Blacks in the ANC, including Nelson Mandela, are mere figureheads. The liberals support Mandela because he is a buffoon. No leader in his right mind offers automatic weapons to 12- and 13-year-olds. Only a sick mind insists that 14-year-old children should vote in national elections. Mandela did in May 1993.

It is now fashionable for the liberal media to blame Buthelezi and Inkatha for all the ills of South Africa while treating Mandela and the ANC like saints at prayer. Inkatha is blamed for the violence; for being "spoilers" in the negotiations. Buthelezi is blamed for reviving Zulu nationalism as though the Zulus ever forgot who they were.

The liberals accuse Buthelezi of collusion with the white so-called right wing. They are angry because he neither seeks the liberals' advice nor their permission. They hate Inkatha because they cannot control it. They deliberately ignore the fact that Buthelezi's and the IFP's sacredly held position has always been that discussions with all political leaders and groups in South Africa are absolutely crucial. To have discussions does not imply acceptance of the policies of a particular leader or group. What willingness to hold talks with all political parties clearly demonstrates is confidence and open-mindedness. Only the liberals find fault with demonstrated confidence and open-mindedness!

Instead of launching sustained campaigns to force the ANC to disband its terrorist army, Umkhonto WeSizwe, or demanding that those responsible for the atrocities in the communist camps in Angola, Uganda, Zambia, and Tanzania be brought to book, the liberals pretend that these are not issues. The ANC is responsible for the deaths of almost three hundred IFP officials, not to mention thousands of supporters. Even young children have been ambushed and massacred while on their way to school simply because their parents belong to IFP. Those responsible for the murders have never been arrested. The liberals are silent on the issue because the victims are black. The liberals are the masters of divide and rule. It is the liberals who concoct phony polls showing that the ANC has majority support among blacks.

Liberals and Conservatives

In South Africa, the Democratic Party is supposedly the home of the liberals. The National Party, the Conservative Party, the *Afrikaner Volksunie* and a host of other smaller parties all represent various versions of conservatism. However, to talk about liberalism and conservatism among white parties in South Africa — even now as they try to recruit black members — is to engage in semantic gymnastics. The Democratic Party, on the one hand, and the National Party and its off-shoots on the other, are two sides of the same coin. They only differ in emphasis and style. The Nationalist group uses forthrightness, while the Democratic Party is cunning and deceptive.

THE CURSE OF MODERN LIBERALISM

Black South Africans are not deceived. If, for example, there were to be an open election in South Africa in which there were only two white candidates, either Zach DeBeer or Frederick Van Zyl Slabbert representing the liberals, running against Eugene Terre Blanche who is considered an extreme "right-winger" by the liberals, Terre Blanche would score a landslide victory. Blacks would vote for Terre Blanche, because they know what to expect from him and therefore how to plan their strategies. If blacks were to vote for DeBeer or Van Zyl Slabbert, they would be gambling with their very lives. To vote for a conservative, on the other hand, would be marching to struggle with eyes open.

Black South Africans distrust "liberal think-tanks" such as the Institute for a Democratic South Africa (IDASA). Apart from the fact that IDASA is a National Party front organization and the liberals who run it are part of South Africa's problem, they seek only to appear progressive without dealing with the difficult issues. They are people of many empty words, words which have different meanings for different situations. Black South Africans have an unchanging response: "We don't trust you."

In South Africa, the liberals are the masters (and mistresses) of "divide and rule." This is the same international liberal policy which helped destroy Africa. The black "elite" are always supported by the liberals in their corruption and abuse of power. They do so in the knowledge that the wealth of black countries does not stay in the countries themselves, but finds its way to banks in foreign lands where the liberals have vested interests. Corrupt black leaders purchase luxury and exotic goods ranging from golden beds to champagne, while their constituents starve to death. The liberal apologists then send aid workers with powdered milk and blankets to take care of the victims of programs enacted by the liberals. Contrary to popular perceptions that liberals are for freedom, modern liberalism is based on manipulation and control.

American Liberals and Black Leaders

Unlike in South Africa, where the liberals, sometimes called moderates, have virtually no chance of ever controlling and manipulating blacks, in the United States the relationship between the white liberal establishment and the black celebrity leadership is an intriguing one. The same U.S. liberal establishment tried to make Tutu and Boesak black South African leaders. That exercise failed dismally. The feverish attempts by the same group to make Mandela a leader is doomed to failure too.

In America, the liberal establishment successfully created a black celebrity leadership — Jesse Jackson, Andrew Young, Coretta Scott King and many of those known as black civil rights leaders. These individuals and groups are the darlings of the liberal establishment. They are also prominent in the Democratic Party. Their function is to keep all blacks in one camp. That is why the overwhelming number of black voters vote for the Democratic Party. Common sense dictates that since they are a minority they should spread themselves between the two parties in order to successfully use the well-known political trick of playing one group against the other.

Sometimes though, the black leadership and the liberal establishment find themselves at odds. The celebrity black leadership has only one potent weapon against the white liberal establishment: the charge of racism.

There is nothing white Americans fear more than being called racists. Black civil rights leaders have mastered the trick. They make white liberals feel guilty enough to take responsibility for what are actually self-inflicted disasters in the black communities. And they do it by simply charging racism. The white liberal establishment responds by wailing and whining and, in the process, gives in even to the most ludicrous demands of the black establishment.

For instance, in the 1980s Randall Robinson and TransAfrica charged that anyone who was against sanctions was pro-apartheid and, therefore, a racist. Nothing is more preposterous. The vast majority of ordinary, hard-working men and women of all races in South Africa opposed to sanctions. Countless legitimate giants of the anti-apartheid struggle including the late Alan Paton, a white lifelong foe of apartheid and a symbol of steadfast courage; the late Bishop Alphaeus Zulu, wise, humble, an unswerving example of Christian compassion in a troubled land; and Chief Mangosuthu Buthelezi, the President of the largest political group in South Africa with a paid-up membership of close to two million. All of these men opposed sanctions. Who among these can be called a racist?

Randall Robinson championed sanctions because it was his livelihood. He had no interest in the people of South Africa. White liberals knew this, but lacked the courage to challenge him. The "1986 Comprehensive Sanctions Act" is a mixture of hypocrisy and foolishness. The sanctions were not even comprehensive. Rather than confront the black leadership with the fact that a weak economy would encourage rather than diminish racism, as the American experience clearly demonstrates, the liberal establishment meekly supported the hypocrisy.

Cynicism and a lack of principle characterize the white liberal establishment. Ask them to spell out clearly just how America's piecemeal and hypocritical sanctions would bring about positive change in South Africa? How would a devastated economy would generate freedom and democracy? How long would it take this panacea to work? What would happen to people who lost their jobs, homes, and educational opportunities, and those who would fall ill for lack of proper nourishment caused by mass poverty? Their rehearsed and recorded answer was that they were responding to calls by "the black leadership." This is the Pontius Pilate syndrome at its worst.

The whole sanctions and disinvestment movement in the U.S. had nothing to do with apartheid. It was an American racial war which was being fought on South African soil, much like U.S./Soviet wars which have been fought in Angola and Afghanistan. The American corporations in South Africa are white-owned corporations. If the black leadership could force them out of South Africa, this would be seen as a major victory against an institution (white corporate America, or big business), which is often accused by the civil rights leaders of being racist, albeit for purposes of extortion. The real fight, therefore, was between the black American leadership and American big business. If the battle against the corporations was won in South Africa then the focus would shift from South Africa to Asia and Latin America. Apartheid existed in South Africa long before the first American corporation established itself there and it would easily survive American sanctions. Black South Africans, for a long time to come, will suffer from divestment and sanctions.

Liberal Hypocrisy

Where was the white liberal voice in Ethiopia when the Eritreans and people of Tigre were butchered by Ethiopians for the past thirty years? Why is the white liberal establishment so concerned about the plight of black South Africans and not concerned at all with Liberia, which was founded by Americans and which has been virtually destroyed by black-on-black violence? Can the expressed concern for blacks ten thousand miles away be genuine? Black South Africans doubt it. And why not, one would ask the liberal establishment — apply sanctions against twenty or so black African states so as to force them to change to democratic rule? Why not impose sanctions against the brutal military regimes in Africa?

Black South Africans want to know why this selective and unbalanced attention? Where is the morality so often claimed by the liberals? This is the real racism. The white liberal establishment is using a different and higher standard to judge white South Africans. There is an unspoken belief that whites should not act like savages or perhaps whites should not legalize oppression as the Afrikaners did. In a sense, the white liberal establishment feels betrayed by the Afrikaners, not because of racism, but because the Afrikaners dared publicize their version of racism. Hence the self-righteous anger at white South Africa. The Afrikaners are a constant reminder to the liberal establishment of racism in America. Shifting attention to apartheid and sanctions swings the spotlight of liberal "conscience" from America to South Africa, but accomplishes nothing.

On the other hand, the white liberal establishment in America today feels the same way Afrikaners felt about blacks two decades ago, namely that they needed to be guided by whites; they could not make it on their own. The Afrikaners were open about this; the liberal establishment in America is not. If the white liberals genuinely accepted the equality of all races, their outrage towards black Africa would equal their outrage against white South Africa. The discrepancy is evidence of classical and deep-seated racism. Oppression is oppression wherever it may appear and lack of freedom is intolerable. But those of us who have either lived in or visited other African states know that the quality of life in apartheid South Africa is infinitely better than anywhere else in black-ruled Africa. The vote is meaningless in black-ruled Africa. I would rather live in South Africa and not vote than live in Somalia, or Liberia, or Uganda, or Sudan, or anywhere else in black Africa and vote. There are several million blacks in South Africa who have escaped, at great risk, from their independent countries where they have the vote, to South Africa where they have a better life without the vote.

The liberal white establishment points a finger at white South Africa not out of concern for blacks there but rather to direct attention from its own failed solutions to racial problems in the U.S. In reaction to the racial upheavals of the 1960s the liberals enacted laws — the Civil Rights Acts and the Voters Act — and put in place such programs as affirmative action, busing, and an elaborate welfare system. Many Americans view affirmative action and busing as "reverse discrimination." Many black Americans see them as failures. The U.S. Supreme Court has found many provisions of "affirmative action" unconstitutional.

Justice or Integration?

Laws cannot solve racial problems; they merely provide a framework or a foundation on which to build lasting healthy race relations. The job of changing people's attitudes is arduous and takes many generations. The idea that integration can be programmed and fostered through busing and affirmative action is ludicrous at best. And the liberals know this. They do not care. They only care about what makes them look good. Their social programs serve as anesthesia which makes them feel good.

The civil rights movement was for justice. However, the white liberal establishment hijacked the movement by making integration the goal. Somehow this goal would be reached through affirmative action and busing. These proved to be nothing more than oases in a desert, where only a few could shelter. The exercise was paternalism at its worst. Blacks were told not just what was good for them, but also how to get it. It was only a matter of time before the myth would explode.

Today, more than a quarter of a century after the passage of the Civil Rights Act, half the black children are born, raised, and die in abject poverty. Too many blacks are born suffering, grow up grumbling, and die disappointed. Blacks account for almost 50 percent of the prison population, although they constitute only 12 percent of the American population. Drugs, violence, and crime kill more blacks than any other population group in the U.S. The black family is becoming an endangered species. The liberal response to all this is that the government must do more.

Many of the mainline churches are heavily influenced by liberal hypocrisy. In 1988 the General Convention of the Episcopal Church, my own church, passed a resolution calling for a boycott of the Shell Oil Company in the U.S.; this because Shell Oil in South Africa allegedly supported apartheid. If such a boycott were to be mounted, tens of thousands of Americans, who have nothing to do with either Shell Oil Company policy in South Africa or with apartheid, would suddenly lose their jobs. Nothing would change in South Africa, because Shell Oil in South Africa is an independent corporation which is not controlled from America. Further, no Shell Oil subsidiary outside South Africa has made any investments there in many years. Black leadership at the 1988 Convention used emotional warfare to get the resolution passed.

The church obviously did not do its homework before deciding on the boycott. Shell Oil corporation is one of the most outstanding and committed corporations in South Africa to ending apartheid. The corporation excels in providing quality education for blacks (especially tutoring them in math, physics, and chemistry), decent modern homes, training in managerial skills, and providing financial support for blacks to start their own businesses. Unlike the pro-sanctions movement, which operated from a paternalistic and self-interested posture, Shell Oil's policy in South Africa has been to consult directly with the black communities around them before initiating any program. Churches could learn a great deal from Shell Oil.

Black South Africans are not surprised when politicians in Congress and other government officials, either in the White House or the U.S. State Department, support the communist-led ANC, despite the trillions of dollars spent fighting communism in the former Soviet Union. Politicians and government officials will support anything and anyone that is in their own best interest. That is why the current U.S. Secretary of State, Warren Christopher, calls Mandela "the hope" for the future, even though Mandela is a communist and a criminal.

Black South Africans have waited in vain for strong condemnation from the liberals for the slaughters of innocent young South Africans in the ANC camps. This issue will remain a festering sore. Many parents, relatives, and loved ones of the slain children are still hoping that the ANC will, through pressure, be forced to account for them.

Calling Jimmy Carter to Account

Nelson Mandela has treated this planned, deliberate, and gross violation of human rights with incredible contempt, dismissing it as an unfortunate minor episode. In December 1991, the Carter Center in Atlanta invited Mandela to be the keynote speaker at a Human Rights Award Ceremony. This was outrageous, given Mandela's own human rights record, and that of the organization of which he is president — the ANC and the terrorist outfit he commands — Umkhonto WeSizwe.

When I learned that Mandela was coming, I tried to get in touch with Mr. Carter by letter, fax, and phone calls to his office. I got no response. Finally, I wrote the following letter to the *Houston Post*, which was published on the day Mandela was to give his speech.

"Mandela is not rights role model"
By Sipo Mzimela
Special to the *Houston Post*:

> Nelson Mandela will be the keynote speaker at a Human Rights Award Ceremony in Houston Sunday. The $100,000 prize was established jointly by former President Jimmy Carter and Dominique de Menil. President Carter will give his annual Human Rights Report at the ceremony.
> The choice of Mandela as keynote speaker is perplexing, given his record on human rights. This record must be examined from two perspectives — namely, that of the organization he leads, the African National Congress (ANC), and his personal pronouncements on the subject.
> As President of the ANC, Mandela leads a Marxist liberation movement that is in a firm alliance with the South African Communist Party. To this day, the ANC has consistently and persistently refused to renounce violence as

THE CURSE OF MODERN LIBERALISM

a means to political goals. Instead, the organization maintains a private army — Umkhonto WeSizwe.

The ANC refuses to surrender its large stockpiles of sophisticated weapons hidden in various parts of South Africa and continues to recruit young black South Africans who are sent for military training in Cuba and Libya — a country the United States says has a record of financing international terrorism. It is the ANC's official commitment to violence that translates into the ongoing senseless and brutal killings in the black townships despite the various peace accords which have been signed.

During his visit to the United States in June last year, Mandela expressed admiration for Yasser Arafat, Fidel Castro, and Moammar Gadhafi. He viewed those three as role models and found nothing wrong with their human rights records. Cuban exiles in Miami were so incensed that Mandela was denied the key to that city.

More important, however, are Mandela's personal remarks he made during an official visit to Cuba last July. During that highly publicized visit, Mandela went out of his way not only to praise Fidel Castro's human-rights record but he denounced Cuban exiles and other critics of Cuba's human-rights violations. Mandela sent shock waves throughout the world when he declared that the disastrous Cuban revolution is a model for South Africa.

Many Cuban exiles are deeply offended by Mandela's pronouncements. Americans of integrity find Mandela's support of Castro and Gadhafi repugnant. Why, then is he giving the keynote address at a human rights award ceremony?

Unless former President Carter and Dominique de Menil give a plausible explanation, their claim to be champions of human rights will be reduced to a political joke. That will be a sad day for the victims of human-rights abusers.

After being honored in Houston by Carter and others, Mandela paid his visit to Teheran where he praised the Islamic Revolution as a model for Africa. He was praising the same people who held American diplomats hostage for over a year.

My warning that Mr. Carter's claim to be a champion of human rights will be reduced to a political joke turned out to be prophetic. In June 1993, Mr. Carter travelled to Vienna, Austria to address a UN-sponsored World Human Rights Conference. When Mr. Carter tried to address the 1,400 strong audience, he was drowned out by a chorus of "Carter, No! Carter, No!" Suffering people around the world are sick and tired of being fooled. Vienna demonstrated that the whole issue of human rights has been reduced to one big political joke. It is indeed a sad development.

The other question still remains unanswered. Why have Mr. Carter and his Center not taken up the issue of the atrocities which were committed by the communist-led ANC, especially at Quatro in Angola?

No doubt, the liberals who possess a bottomless reservoir of nice-sounding words have an answer, but until their deeds are convincing, black South Africans will never trust them.

Chapter 8

Inkatha Freedom Party

The decision to break all ties with the ANC after the organization merged with the South African Communist Party in 1985, was a very difficult one for me. I had been a member for 33. My parents and grandparents had been members. The roots ran deep.

On the other hand, I could not bring myself to accept that once again in history blacks had been outmaneuvered by whites into accepting slavery. The thought that the organization I had been so proud of had been taken over by communists was too painful. I could picture Joseph Slovo and his fellow travelers joking about the "stupid blacks" who had been conned into marching gleefully to slavery.

For five years, from 1985 to 1990, I turned my back on politics. I even seriously considered becoming a U.S. citizen and forgetting South Africa altogether. I went so far as getting the necessary application forms. In the end, however, I decided against such a move and opted instead to work towards improved educational standards for black South Africans.

In 1990, when I returned to South Africa after 29 years in exile, I traveled to Ulundi, to visit Chief Mangosuthu Buthelezi. I first met Dr. Buthelezi in 1953 when he came to worship at our church, St. Faith's Anglican Church in Durban. He was in the company of other members of the Zulu royal family. He too was a member of the ANC.

After he formed Inkatha in 1975, he visited New York, where I was deputy representative of the ANC. I always met with him. I never considered him an enemy just because he formed a rival political organization. In fact, until 1980, we ANC representatives abroad were under instructions never to attack homeland leaders. In 1980, Oliver Tambo, who was president of the ANC, instructed me to approach fellow Anglican Desmond Tutu and request him to refrain from attacking Buthelezi in the South African press.

After my visit with Buthelezi in June 1990, I decided to return to active politics under the banner of Inkatha. That same year Inkatha became a political party — Inkatha Freedom Party (IFP). The way the IFP and Dr. Buthelezi are treated in the South African and international popular media defies reason.

In the play "Julius Caesar," William Shakespeare wrote: "The evil that men do lives after them, the good is oft interred with their bones."

This is turned upside down for some people in South Africa. The evil that they do is interred while they live and they are celebrated by the liberal media as heroes and martyrs. So it is with Nelson Mandela. He is Xhosa.

For others, the good they do is interred while they live and they are cast as villains of the deepest dye by the same media. So it is with Dr. Mangosuthu Buthelezi. He is Zulu.

Zulu Politics

No nation in the history of South Africa has lost more people fighting for their rights, freedom, and sovereignty than the Zulu nation. No other people in South Africa have been the object of more blatant ridicule by the liberal media than the Zulus.

No other political party in South Africa has been so deliberately misrepresented in the liberal media both in South Africa and abroad as Inkatha Freedom Party. No other political leader has been consistently and persistently vilified by the liberal establishment as Dr. Mangosuthu Buthelezi, president of Inkatha Freedom Party and chief minister of KwaZulu.

Anti-Zuluism is relatively new in the U.S. It is the product of the vicious anti-Zulu propaganda spread by Randall Robinson and TransAfrica, the Congressional Black Caucus, the civil rights leaders and, of course, the liberal media establishment. In South Africa, anti-Zuluism has old and deep roots. Many have not forgiven the Zulus for refusing to dance to the tunes of the former British Empire.

To many liberals, Dr. Buthelezi is a constant reminder of mighty Zulu kings — Shaka, Dingane, Cetshwayo and Dinizulu. Buthelezi is their descendent. His political consistency, like that of his ancestors, is a thorn in their side. Unlike Mandela, they can neither manipulate nor buy him.

As mentioned earlier, Inkatha Yenkululeko Yesizwe (Inkatha) was founded as a political movement by Dr. Buthelezi in 1975 to promote unity among black oppressed South Africans and to thwart the apartheid regime's grand design of confining blacks in ethnic homelands, where they would be reduced to the status of slaves.

In the 1970s, Inkatha was formed to save South Africa from self-destruction. The Xhosa of the Transkei and Ciskei, the Venda of Venda, and the Tswana of Bophuthatswana, accepted "independence" from Pretoria. But the Zulus, under the leadership of Dr. Buthelezi, refused to be squeezed out of the country. Dr. Buthelezi, in particular, earned the wrath of the South African government for daring to scuttle its grand apartheid design. With eight million Zulus, the largest nation in South Africa — refusing to go along with government plans, cracks began to appear in what had been considered apartheid's impenetrable wall. Buthelezi paid dearly for his stand. The government confiscated his passport and denied him for nine years the right to travel.

At one time the arrogant P.W. Botha, who was then president of South Africa, threatened Buthelezi and wagged his fingers at him as though he were a little boy. Today, P.W.

Botha has fallen from his false throne and has become a nonentity. Buthelezi continues on his march to victory.

Contrary to anti-Zulu media propaganda, Buthelezi has never viewed the struggle of the Zulus as something separate and distinct from the total liberation of all the oppressed in South Africa. Like the ANC of old, he has always wanted all the oppressed to unite, overthrow apartheid, and replace it with democracy. To that end, he helped form the Black Alliance, which brought together the political leadership of all the disenfranchised groups in South Africa — black, colored, and Indian. The South African government accused him of promoting the aims and objectives of the banned ANC. This was a serious charge, but Buthelezi was not intimidated, although that is exactly what he was doing.

When he formed Inkatha Yenkulueko Yesizwe (Inkatha) in 1975, he really resurrected the original African National Congress (ANC). The ANC's founding father, Pixley Ka Isaka Seme, was his uncle. When Dr. Seme, a graduate of Columbia University in New York, and others formed the ANC in 1912, they were convinced that only peaceful action would liberate blacks in South Africa from the tyranny of white oppression. Their conviction was rooted in the bitter experiences of many brutal wars, especially between the Zulus and the Afrikaners and between the Zulus and the British. After the Zulus lost the last war in 1906, Seme prophesied:

> "The brighter day is rising upon Africa. Already I seem to see her chains dissolve, her desert plains red with harvest, her Abyssinia and her Zululand the seats of science and religion.... all her sons employed in advancing the victories of peace.... greater and more abiding than the spoils of war."

However, the awesome growth of white military and economic power in South Africa seemed to turn Seme's "brighter day" into eternal darkness. When the ANC was banned in 1960, a few within the ANC concluded that there would never be "victories of peace," and opted instead for "the spoils of war." Thus, the so-called armed struggle was launched, allegedly under the banner of the ANC.

The Struggle for Non-Violence

By 1975, the communist-led ANC and the South African government firmly believed in brutal violence as the means of either gaining or maintaining political power. However, not all South African political leaders were disciples of violence.

For example, Dr. Seme's powerful message of peaceful change was not lost on Buthelezi. It was clear to him that both the ANC and the South African government were hell-bent on leading South Africa into a conflict where there could be no winners.

Conflict can either be settled violently by eliminating one's opponent, or peacefully by accommodating opposing views. Buthelezi chose accommodation. He called on all South Africans to adopt peaceful negotiation as the strategy for resolving South Africa's myriad problems.

To Buthelezi's dismay, people of goodwill, inside and outside South Africa, didn't rally behind his call for nonviolence. Instead, he was vilified, scorned, insulted, and derided as a "sell-out," "puppet," and "Uncle Tom." He, alone among black leaders in South Africa, was targeted for assassination by the ANC. The South African government tried its best to topple him as chief minister of KwaZulu because he refused to bow down to its sham demands of making KwaZulu an independent state. Buthelezi would not go away. He steadfastly refused to negotiate with the South African government until Nelson Mandela and all political prisoners were released from prison. To the utter dismay of the ANC, he refused to negotiate until all banned organizations were unbanned. Even as the ANC was plotting to assassinate him, he was fighting its battles, not on distant international platforms, but amid the real heat: the corridors of awesome white power inside South Africa.

The white South African liberal establishment — the lords and ladies of paternalism — grew increasingly irritated with Buthelezi, because he refused to be their toy. He knew that the vast majority of oppressed people in South Africa wanted peaceful change. He knew that the liberal establishment only wanted an appearance of being on the right side and, therefore, could not be trusted.

The ANC responded to Buthelezi's call for negotiated peaceful change by throwing young black children into the battlefield after telling them to "choose liberation before education" and "make South Africa ungovernable." Children went on the rampage, burning down their own schools, libraries, laboratories, and community centers. When they did go to school, it was for strictly Marxist political education. Today, thanks to the ANC, six million black youths are illiterate. They are known as "the Lost Generation," brutalized, dehumanized, and criminalized.

Inkatha countered this senseless destruction of the black youth by stressing "education for liberation."

In 1979, ANC and Inkatha leaders met in London to formulate a common black strategy to fight apartheid. The meeting failed for three reasons. First, the ANC wanted to direct the struggle inside South Africa from its headquarters outside the country in Lusaka, Zambia. Second, Inkatha rejected the so-called armed struggle on grounds that South African blacks had already fought and lost too many wars against whites. Finally, Inkatha also rejected economic sanctions against South Africa, because the country has only one economy in which both blacks and whites must prosper or perish. Damaging that economy would hurt blacks more than whites, since blacks possessed fewer resources.

After the failure of the London meeting, the ANC declared all black South Africans who refused to adopt its strategy of violence to be its enemies and, therefore, fair game. This meant that Inkatha had become the ANC's number one target. What was supposed to be a war of liberation from apartheid became black-on-black violence.

Some members of Inkatha, even though still professing nonviolence, were sucked into the violence, only to be accused by the ANC of collaborating with the South African government, police, and secret branches of the security forces. Inkatha officials were targeted for murder by the communists. To date, almost three hundred officials have been murdered.

An international liberal media campaign to paint Inkatha as an arm of the South African government was launched, making strange bedfellows indeed: the world communist empire, the international white liberal establishment, brutal African regimes, and the black American civil rights leaders. Parties of this unholy alliance portrayed the ANC as the "sole legitimate representative of all black South Africans." The ANC boldly proclaimed to the world that it was a government-in-waiting. Inkatha, which refused to change its policy on nonviolence, was labelled a surrogate of the South African government. It was all a sham.

From the mid-'80s violence in the black townships escalated and claimed thousands of black lives. The violence led to loss of confidence on the part of investors, which in turn led to economic decline, just as Inkatha had predicted.

Finally in February 1990, President F.W. de Klerk conceded that his party's scheme of white supremacy could never work in South Africa, nor could his government succeed in maintaining apartheid through force. Apartheid had to go. Thus, Buthelezi's disarming consistency and abiding integrity paid off.

On February 2, 1990, de Klerk announced from Parliament in Cape Town that his government would take steps to "normalize" the political climate in South Africa. Free political activity would take place, leading to a negotiated settlement, a new constitution, and a new democratically-elected government.

Towards the end of his speech to Parliament and the world on February 2, 1990, de Klerk had this to say:

> "To those political leaders who have always resisted violence, I say thank you for your principled stands. This includes all the leaders of parliamentary parties, leaders of important organizations and movements, such as Chief Minister Buthelezi, all of the other Chief Ministers, and urban community leaders.
>
> "Through their participation and discussion they have made an important contribution to this moment in which the process of free political participation is able to be restored. Their places in the negotiating process are assured."

The media scornfully refers to Inkatha as "a Zulu-based movement" or "a conservative Zulu movement," in spite of Inkatha's representative cross-section of South Africa's ethnic and cultural groups. The same media never refer to the ANC as "a Xhosa-based movement" or "a communist-led movement." Nor are any of the white parties referred to as "the English-based Democratic Party" or "the Afrikaner-based National Party." Only Inkatha is singled out for distortion and attack by the liberal media.

De Klerk's speech to parliament was a bitter pill for the ANC to swallow. Its guerrilla army became the first and only one in the history of armed struggle in Africa to become obsolete without ever having engaged its enemy in battle. All the bragging of 30 years about seizing power came to nothing. The big lie of those who went around the world sporting expensive suits and collecting millions of dollars by saying that the "ANC's military wing" was engaged in combat inside South Africa, was exposed by de Klerk's February 2, 1990 speech.

The braggarts were forced to go cap in hand to de Klerk to ask that their disgraced fighters be allowed to return home and not die in exile. In 30 long years of "armed struggle," they had captured not even one square inch of South African land. There was never an armed struggle, only terrorism against unarmed civilians, mostly blacks.

For 15 years, Buthelezi had rejected violence and, against Herculean odds, called for a negotiated settlement of South Africa's political problems. For him personally, and for Inkatha, the 2nd of February, 1990, will go down in history as a day of great triumph. South Africa would now be changed through negotiations. The media never acknowledged the significance of this.

The Media and the ANC

Instead, the media created an ANC victory. Mandela's release a week later, which Buthelezi had long demanded from the government as a pre-condition for beginning negotiations, was portrayed as Mandela's doing. If Buthelezi had agreed to reach a settlement without Mandela, the ANC communists would still be in exile and Mandela would still be in jail. This was not deemed newsworthy. Mandela thanked Buthelezi for his efforts by refusing to meet with him for eleven months. Mandela did visit Yassir Arafat and Moammar Gadhafi.

For months following the February 2nd speech, the media treated the world to a steady dose of misinformation and disinformation. Every meeting between Mandela and de Klerk or their delegations was treated by the media as a major step towards handing power over to the ANC. It appeared that only the government and the ANC were involved in the negotiations. In an effort to neutralize Inkatha, the ANC intensified its campaign of intimidation and violence, while accusing Inkatha of collusion with the police and army. The international media had a field day.

As the ANC became more confident that it was about to take over South Africa, it announced in July 1990, that it would dismantle KwaZulu, the traditional home of the Zulus. Mandela and other top ANC functionaries hobnobbed with corrupt Xhosa dictators in the Transkei. These men were the real collaborators with apartheid who abandoned their black brothers and sisters to apartheid while they accepted sham independence. That is something Buthelezi and Inkatha resolutely refuse to do.

Instead of acknowledging Buthelezi's principled stand, the ANC leadership singled out Buthelezi and the Zulu nation for ridicule and vilification. This was a mistake the ANC will never be allowed to forget. If the Zulu leadership had responded to the ANC challenge by calling on the Zulus to destroy the ANC it would have been annihilated in a matter of days. It is a measure of maturity and statesmanship that, in spite of extreme and unprovoked acts of provocation and terror, the Inkatha and Zulu leadership counseled restraint. The foolish attempts to destroy KwaZulu failed. Once again, Buthelezi, Inkatha, and the Zulu nation insisted that South Africa's complex problems could not be solved by thuggery and terrorism. They can only be solved by genuine negotiations based on mutual respect and tolerance.

The efforts to topple Buthelezi and destroy Inkatha did not end in July 1990. In fact, the communist-led ANC's primary objective is not working for democracy in South Africa, but for the destruction of Inkatha and Buthelezi. This objective took a decisive turn in July 1991.

"Inkathagate"

Every year in July, tens of thousands of party delegates from across South Africa gather under giant tents for Inkatha's annual conference. They come by bus, train, car, on foot, and a lucky few by air. The local schools are turned into dormitories where the delegates sleep on hard concrete floors. Some are accommodated in the homes of party members and friends. Only a few find accommodation in what is the smallest Holiday Inn in the world; the only hotel in Ulundi.

Old men and women who can neither read nor write, but who display dignity which defies description, come from many villages around the country. They mingle easily with young executives and professionals from Johannesburg, Durban, Cape Town, Pretoria, and smaller towns.

THE INKATHA FREEDOM PARTY

The 1991 conference was special. It was the first one since Inkatha had become a multi-racial political party in December 1990. Until that time Inkatha had been a black nonviolent liberation movement. Many white delegates were in attendance for the first time. They came from affluent Sandton in Johannesburg. There were also Zulu-speaking white farmers from across Natal, Afrikaners from Stellenbosch, the heart of Afrikanerdom, and Pretoria, the seat of Afrikaner power. There were Asian and colored delegations as well.

The air was full of excitement and anticipation, as well as a sense of triumph, even though the liberal media tried to ignore it. Chief Buthelezi had just completed his historic visit with President Bush. As a result of the trip, American sanctions had been lifted against South Africa and her athletes were readmitted into the Olympic games. The ANC conference in Durban a few days earlier had ended with the adoption of the same old rhetorical positions which could only lead the country to disaster. All eyes were now on Inkatha.

The day before the conference opened, *The Weekly Mail*, a white liberal publication of neither standing nor influence, published an article claiming that Inkatha had been funded by the government. There was an immediate international chain reaction from the liberal media. Inkatha Freedom Party (IFP) was now accused of being a creation of the South African government. Without facts or proof, the liberal press in South Africa and abroad went into a frenzy.

On Friday, July 19th, the Inkatha Central Committee, which includes representatives from across the country, as well as representatives from the Youth and Women's Brigades, met on schedule at 8:00 p.m. When I left at 12:15 a.m. there was still no sign that the meeting was going to end. Yet in all that time, not a word had been spoken about the slanderous reports in the newspapers. When I asked an old hand about the non-reaction, he said simply, "We are used to this."

It was my duty and honor to open the conference with devotions the next morning. In my homily, which was based on the Sermon on the Mount, I touched on the current efforts to discredit Inkatha. However, no one seemed overly concerned, even though most of the South African papers were beginning to make a major issue of the report in *The Weekly Mail*.

The mood changed dramatically on Sunday morning. South African liberal journalists claimed, in screaming headlines, that Inkatha was "mortally wounded," "exposed," and "gasping for breath." The Johannesburg *Sunday Times* called on Inkatha delegates to get rid of Buthelezi and elect Dr. Oscar Dhlomo, former General Secretary of Inkatha, in his place. Liberal racists have always claimed for themselves the right to tell blacks what to do and blacks are supposed to obey without question.

"Inkathagate" was a carefully planned media event designed to deal the Inkatha Freedom Party a mortal blow. It was a follow-up to the July 1990 attempt by the ANC to destroy Inkatha, the Zulu nation, and Chief Buthelezi. Journalists had selected what they thought would be an ideal time to "explode the bomb," thinking the assembled delegates were pliable. They assumed the many new white delegates would be disgusted and leave Inkatha.

Even officials of the almost defunct white Democratic Party called on Buthelezi to resign. In a brilliant and appropriate move, Buthelezi confidently requested that the legitimate delegates deal with the situation. Twenty-two thousand delegates sat in stunned silence as they listened to the accusations leveled at their party and leaders. We could have heard a pin drop. For those of us who have lived too long in the West and are always in a hurry, it was marvelous to observe African patience at work. The only thunderous indignation erupted when the articles calling for Buthelezi's replacement were read. In the uproar, one could hear some real obscenities being hurled at the journalists. The chairman of Inkatha Freedom Party, Dr. Frank Mdlalose rose to his feet and asked for order.

At the end of it all, Buthelezi asked the delegates to decide whether or not he had to resign. He said, "If you feel I have disgraced and failed you, tell me to *voetsek* and I will leave." *Voetsek* is an Afrikaans word normally used to tell dogs to "get out."

Somebody started chanting *"Shenge, Shenge"* and within seconds everything seemed to move in rhythm as the crowds thundered "*Shenge! Shenge! Shenge!*" — the name that Buthelezi's followers and friends affectionately call him. Anyone who knows African culture would know that song was soon to follow. And so, almost automatically, the assembled thousands broke into song; into Inkatha's song of commitment: *"Baya le, baya le siyaphambili"* ("They go hither, they go thither. We are marching forward.")

The harmony was so incredibly rich that I concluded that angels had joined in the singing. With arms stretched towards heaven, some cried while others laughed. Buthelezi was lifted shoulder-high. Dr. Mdlalose made his way to the microphone and bellowed: "Who is our leader?" The crown thundered back "*Shenge!*" Inkathagate was dead and buried. The three-hour event turned out to be one of the most memorable in the history of politics in South Africa. The South African press and the international media chose to pretend nothing newsworthy had happened.

What Really Happened

In 1988, after relentless intimidation and violent attacks on Inkatha supporters, Inkatha leadership established an anonymous bank account. Inkatha even published the account number so that those wishing to make financial contributions to Inkatha could do so anonymously. In its 15-year history Inkatha had held hundreds of rallies, but two conferences came under public scrutiny because the South African Ministry of Foreign Affairs, without the knowledge of Inkatha leadership, had helped finance the rallies by contributing to the secret bank account. As a result, false reports and media coverage claimed that the IFP was being funded by the South African government.

One of the rallies in question was, in fact, an *Imbizo* (Zulu word for convocation) which was called by His Majesty the King of the Zulus in November 1989. The second rally in March 1990, was a thanksgiving meeting, which was more of a religious service than a political rally. Buthelezi had called for the rally to give thanks to God for the release of Nelson Mandela and other political prisoners, as well as for the unbanning of the ANC, the PAC, and the SACP. The ANC and its white liberal supporters used an act of good will on the part of Inkatha to try to create a scandal.

It must be emphasized that the South African Ministry of Foreign Affairs contributed exactly $88,339.22 to the fund to help in the fight against sanctions, something Inkatha had opposed from its inception. Neither Dr. Buthelezi nor the Central committee of Inkatha Freedom Party knew of the contribution.

However, since the special fund had been set up to do humanitarian work (which included providing for the victims of ANC violence) and not to fight sanctions, Inkatha refunded the money in full. M.Z. Khumalo, the Inkatha official who knew about the funding, acted in good faith, but without authorization. Above all, Inkatha feels no shame. The party did nothing wrong.

Why did the white liberal press and the fast-fading Democratic Party call on Buthelezi to resign? Buthelezi never asked for the money, nor did he know that it had been paid into the anonymous account. De Klerk's officials were responsible for the whole affair. De Klerk was not asked to resign. Buthelezi was.

An observation: The ANC has received financial gifts over the years from the Soviet Empire, Gadhafi, Afarat, Castro, North Korea, Vietnam, the Scandinavia countries, the United States, and Canada exceeding half a billion dollars. Apart from making the ANC hierarchy rich, the money has been used to purchase arms in order to destroy South Africa and to cause untold suffering and misery among blacks. Half a billion dollars never attracted the attention of the media, but $88,000 did.

Perhaps *The Weekly Mail* can tell the world how much the ANC has spent so far on gasoline, tires, and matches, in order to incinerate political opponents. From that, we might be able to figure out how much the movement will spend when it runs the interim government, since, at that stage, it will be crucial to eliminate all opposition. Elections will never be needed again. To the ANC communists, "interim government" is a euphemism for seizure of power.

"Inkathagate" turned out to be a bonanza for Buthelezi and Inkatha. Buthelezi received a unanimous and resounding vote of confidence from the delegates who saw the whole affair for what it really was, one more futile attempt by the ANC and white liberals to destroy Inkatha. Delegates left the conference determined to return to their respective areas to work diligently for an all-out Inkatha victory at the polls. They were not to be deterred by an attacking press.

If Inkatha were weak and a mere tool of the government, surely there would be no need for the ANC, its liberal backers, and large sections of the South African liberal press to launch a relentless and vicious anti-Inkatha, anti-Zulu campaign.

What Inkatha Freedom Party Stands For:

In December 1990, Inkatha transformed itself into a fully fledged political party — Inkatha Freedom Party (IFP) and set itself four basic tasks. They are:

Task 1: To establish an open, free, non-racial, equal opportunity, reconciled society with democratic safeguards for all people.

Task 2: To harness the great resources of the country to fight the real enemies of the people, namely poverty, hunger, unemployment, disease, ignorance, insecurity, homelessness, and moral decay.

Task 3: To ensure a fair distribution of the wealth of the country for the benefit of all people, and to establish political and economic structures that encourage enterprise and create wealth all governments of the future will need.
Task 4: To ensure the maintenance of a stable, peaceful society in which people can pursue their happiness and realize their potential without fear or favour.

These are noble tasks which demonstrate a vision apparent in no other political party in South Africa. This vision can satisfy the needs and allay the justified fears of the majority of South Africans.

When the goals of the communist-controlled ANC are compared to those of the Inkatha Freedom Party, it is quite clear who truly stands for South African ideals.

The Communist-controlled ANC

- A Marxist liberation movement.
- Believes in violence as a means to political goals.
- Has a private army and continues to train new recruits in Uganda, Libya, Cuba, and India.
- Has large stockpiles of sophisticated weapons hidden inside South Africa and other countries.
- Wants to seize power through the establishment of an interim government and constituent assembly.
- Wants a centralized all-controlling government amounting to a dictatorship.
- Ignores the legitimacy of cultural differences.
- Wants a phony bill of rights based on its Marxist Freedom Charter.
- Enslaved to the completely discredited central command economic system based on Marxism.
- Will nationalize mines, banks, and so-called monopoly industries.
- Committed to redistribution of wealth, i.e., taking from the rich and giving to the poor.

- Draws almost all its financial support from outside South Africa, especially from Cuba, Libya, North Korea, America, and Scandinavia.
- Supported the Soviet invasions of Czechoslovakia and Afghanistan, and opposed Gorbachev's reforms.
- Close allies with Yassir Arafat of the PLO and highly critical of Israel.
- Supported Saddam Hussein before, during, and after the Gulf War. Highly critical of the USA.
- Is an atheistic, revolutionary movement.

Inkatha Freedom Party

- A democratic multi-cultural party.
- Believes in nonviolence as a means to political goals.
- Has no army and no trainees.
- Has no stockpiles of arms anywhere.
- Wants to participate in the drafting of a democratic constitution which will lead to democratic elections for a democratic government.
- Wants a strong decentralized government structure with very limited central government control.
- Accepts the reality and legitimacy of cultural differences and seeks to protect minorities.
- Wants a strong and comprehensive Bill of Rights (A Charter of Individual Rights and Responsibilities) based on the principle of natural freedoms (God-given Rights).
- Wants a democratic economic system based on the principles of free enterprise.
- Will leave the running of business to the private sector and will concentrate on managing the country.
- Believes in the creation of wealth and the distribution of opportunities.
- Most of its financial support is from its membership inside South Africa.

- Have always opposed invasions and, as early as May 1991, supported resolutions calling for the independence of the Baltic States.
- Supports Middle East peace based on unconditional acceptance of Israel's right to exist within safe and secure borders. Finds the idea that Israel has no right to exist repugnant.
- Supported the allies in the Gulf War.
- Includes members of many different faiths but is fundamentally a Christian movement.

The South African and international liberal media arrogantly and stubbornly refer to IFP as a "Zulu-based movement." The simple and indisputable fact is that the IFP is a multiracial, multi-ethnic political party. At last count the IFP membership was 58 percent Zulu and 42 percent non-Zulu. South Africans of all races realize that the National Party of F.W. de Klerk has sold out to the communist-led ANC. And Mandela has sold out blacks to white communists in the hope that they will allow him to become the first black president of South Africa. So the party is growing by leaps and bounds.

Just as the original Inkatha thwarted the National Party's grand design of apartheid, so does Inkatha Freedom Party now stand as the only bulwark against the communist-led ANC's agenda.

Contrary to Western arrogance, the practice of government by the people preceded the arrival of white colonialists in South Africa. Whites, through apartheid, replaced the African tradition and introduced dictatorship and racism to South Africa.

When the leadership of Inkatha Freedom Party insists that the new South Africa must be a multi-party democracy with a free-market economy, a bill of rights, and a federal system of government, it gives a modern interpretation to what is indigenous to South Africa. The IFP leadership is not relying solely on the political philosophy of John Locke, although he is very important to us. It is not trying to plant foreign concepts in South African soil. The IFP seeks to combine what is natural among the various black ethnic groups, with the best Asia and Europe have to offer.

On the other hand, the Indian and white ANC communists want to force communism on the people of South Africa.

The history of post-colonial Africa, shows why democracy failed to take root in the former European colonies. The independent African states were virtually given copies of Western constitutions and told to model their countries on Europe. It is much more like draining the lake and expecting the fish to live.

For the new South Africa to become a functioning democracy the best of what is indigenous to the black ethnic groups of South Africa must be combined with the best from Asia and Europe. As things stand now, only the program of Inkatha Freedom Party offers that combination.

Chapter 9

CODESA
The Congress for a Democratic South Africa

On December 20, 1991, the long-awaited Convention for a Democratic South Africa (CODESA) convened at the World Trade Center in Johannesburg. The first sessions were scheduled for December 20 and 21, 1991 and the second for May 15 and 16, 1992. The stated purpose of CODESA was to lay the foundation for a new democratic South Africa. The word "democracy" was on every delegate's lips.

Modern South Africa has neither a tradition nor a culture of democracy. As a result, the concept of democracy has different meanings for different groups. CODESA itself was undemocratic in spirit and in fact. It was condemned to serious difficulties from the very beginning.

It all started with the opening remarks of the Chief Justice of South Africa, Chief Justice Corbett. This is what he said in his opening remarks:

> What we are witnessing today at this opening session of CODESA is history in the making, and I think that it is appropriate that I should for a brief moment turn back the pages of history to Monday, 12 October, 1908. For it was on that day that the National Union Convention, comprising representatives from the four colonies, the Cape, the Transvaal, the Orange Free State, and Natal, together with an observer delegation from what was then Southern Rhodesia, met for the first time in Durban to discuss the formation of a political union and to draw up a draft constitution.

Coincidentally, it was nine years to the day after the outbreak of the Anglo-Boer War. The chairman of the convention was the distinguished Sir Henry de Villiers, then the Chief Justice of the Cape Colony and later to become the first Chief Justice of the Union of South Africa. In opening the Convention, Sir Henry emphasised the difficulties which would be encountered, but stated that he was confident that they would not prove to be insurmountable. He continued and I quote:

"Everything depends upon the spirit with which we approach the performance of our task. Failure is certain if we start with a feeling of distrust and suspicion of each other and with the sole desire to secure as many advantages as we can for our respective political parties or our respective colonies. Success is certain if we give to each other our fullest confidence and act upon the principle that while not neglectful of the interests of those who have sent us here, we are for the time being representatives of the whole of South Africa. A great opportunity now lies before us and it is an opportunity which may not soon occur again."

The conference Chief Justice Corbett referred to is the one hated by all black South Africans. It was the all-white, racist conference which laid the foundation for the Union of South Africa and, by extension, apartheid. Chief Justice Corbett showed total disregard for the feelings of the black delegates at CODESA and those of the 30 million black victims of apartheid — a system which the South African judicial system helped to perpetuate. CODESA got off to a very bad start.

Undemocratic Talks on Democracy

Nineteen political parties and organizations were represented at CODESA I and II. However, the way the representation was weighted reveals how undemocratic CODESA was. The Indians, who number less than one million out of the total population of 38 million, had three delegations representing four political parties — The National People's Party, Solidarity Party, Natal Indian Congress, and Transvaal Indian Congress. Whites, who number five million, were also represented by three delegations. The white-led SACP, which has only 3,000 members, had its own delegation. The various black ethnic groups — Tswanas, Vendas, Swazis, Ndebeles — each had one delegation, but the Xhosa's had two delegations — Transkei and Ciskei. The Zulus, who number eight million out of 38 million, were denied any representation by the ANC/SACP/South African Government Alliance. Some at CODESA seriously believed the Zulus could be forced to accept decisions to which they were not party. How different was this from apartheid, which excluded blacks from decision-making?

Also disturbing was the lack of integrity on the part of the judges who chaired the proceedings; Justice Shabort and the Indian judge, Justice Mahomed. At CODESA I in December 1991, Justice Shabort claimed that the delegations would speak alphabetically. Delegates later found out that the ANC/SACP Alliance and the South African government had privately agreed that the ANC would speak first and the South African government last. If the delegations had spoken alphabetically, the Ximoko Progressive Party of Gazankulu would have spoken last and not the South African government.

Justice Mohamed was even more blatant in his support for the ANC/SACP. In introducing Chris Hani, the SACP's General Secretary, he made the preposterous claim that Chris Hani "has a reputation both for classical scholarship and military strategy." Chris Hani's only reputation had was that of a murderer. Justice Mohamed also had the temerity to refer to President de Klerk and Nelson Mandela as the "joint" architects of CODESA; this when seventeen other parties had worked tirelessly to make it happen. Mohamed also gave Mandela extra time at the closing of the day to deliver what turned out to be a vicious attack on President de Klerk.

Mohamed claimed that Mandela had "earned" extra time to speak.

At the end of CODESA I, Mohamed, supporting of his claim that the architects of CODESA were the government and the ANC, lied to the delegates and said, "I have had a special request in the last few minutes from two speakers of great stature. They are the State President, Mr. de Klerk, and Dr. Nelson Mandela." The so-called "requests" were for closing speeches. Mandela, the opportunist, inevitably seized the moment to babble. When de Klerk's turn came, he immediately announced to the obviously surprised delegates that he had made no request to speak.

Many of us at CODESA I who had seen communist tactics for taking control concluded that Mohamed was taking his instructions from the ANC/SACP Alliance. If officials such as Mohamed, who are entrusted with the administration of justice, cannot be impartial and honest, democracy will not take root in South Africa. Apart from his ANC/SACP leanings, Mohamed, throughout the proceedings, was intoxicated with imaginary self-importance, which translated into irrelevant, flowery verbosity.

CODESA was unrepresentative for other reasons, too. The white Conservative Party and the Afrikaner Resistance Movement were not there. Neither were the black Pan Africanist Congress and Azapo represented. They chose not to participate in what they rightly saw as an exercise in futility.

CODESA I set up five working groups on various issues in preparation for CODESA II. Agreement was to be reached in these committees not through majority vote, but by a nebulous mechanism known as "sufficient consensus." No one in South Africa has a precise definition of "sufficient consensus." Deadlock was inevitable. "Sufficient consensus" did finally lead to two blocks of alliances within CODESA: a communist-led block bent on transforming South Africa into a one-party communist state; and those parties which want the new South Africa to be a multiparty, free-enterprise democracy.

The former still believed in violent revolution and had grandiose ideas of "overthrowing" the present South African government before the end of 1992. The latter group believe in negotiations which will lead to the establishment of democracy, freedom, prosperity and peace for all South Africans.

It became quite clear at CODESA I that the Stalinist ANC/SACP Alliance had not come to "negotiate," but rather to dictate. They were present to give the terms for a transfer of power from a white minority government to a black majority one. The ANC/SACP viewed CODESA as a forum to endorse the archaic Freedom Charter, which had been drawn up by a congress dominated by communists in Kliptown, near Johannesburg in 1955. The misnamed Freedom Charter remains the ANC/SACP sacred constitution.

Many delegations at CODESA were uneasy about the ANC/SACP's ability to abide by the tentative agreements reached. Since the unbanning of the ANC in February 1990, the organization has signed several agreements, most of them designed to end the senseless violence in South Africa and create a climate conducive to negotiations, leading to lasting peace and stability. Those agreements are:

1. The Groote Schuur Minute signed between the government and the ANC in Cape Town on May 2, 1990;
2. The agreement signed between the ANC and Inkatha Freedom Party in Durban on January 29, 1991;
3. The D.F. Malan Accord signed between the government and the ANC in Cape Town on February 12, 1991;
4. The Pretoria Minute signed between the government and the ANC in Pretoria on August 6, 1991;
5. The National Peace Accord which the ANC signed on September 14, 1991.

The ANC has violated the spirit and letter of each of these accords in turn by:

1. Refusing to renounce violence as a means to political ends;

2. By refusing to disband their so-called military wing, Umkhonto WeSizwe (MK) and their criminal MBOKODO;
3. By refusing to surrender all arms caches inside South Africa;
4. Continuing to recruit young black South Africans for terrorist training in Uganda and Libya;
5. Continuing to intimidate and burn to death political opponents;
6. Using inflammatory language designed to incite violence.

Mandela and De Klerk at Each Other's Throats

Even though Mandela and de Klerk had secretly agreed to manipulate CODESA in their favor, like all robbers, they did not trust each other. De Klerk wanted to speak last so that he could attack the ANC/SACP and get away with it. That is how robbers operate. Obviously he needs some education on how communists operate. In his speech, de Klerk said:

> "Mr. Chairman, from the Government's point of view, there is one major obstacle in the way of rapid progress with CODESA. I regret having to refer to it here, but that is, unfortunately, unavoidable. It has to do with the lack of progress by the ANC in coming into line with other political parties and movements. It appears to wish to remain different.
>
> "The heart of the problem is the following: The ANC has not yet terminated what it has itself defined as the "armed struggle."
>
> "In this connection, the ANC has not honored important undertakings in terms of the Pretoria Minute and the D.F. Malan Conference and has resorted to delaying tactics.
>
> "Before the Peace Conference on the 14th of September, 1991, I considered making the solution of this important problem, which includes disclosure of illegal

arms caches within the Republic of South Africa, a pre-condition for signing the Peace Accord. In view of renewed undertakings at that stage by the ANC, I refrained from doing so.

"Unfortunately, this concession did not produce results. As we are gathered here, there still has not been sufficient progress in spite of ongoing efforts on the part of the Government.

"The stipulation in the Peace Accord that no political party shall have a private army places a question mark over the ANC's participation in a convention which, essentially, is taking place among political parties.

"An organization which remains committed to an armed struggle cannot be trusted completely when it also commits itself to peacefully negotiated solutions. Everything that is happening in the world today proves that violence and peaceful compromise are not compatible. The choice is between peace through negotiation or a power struggle through violence. The ANC and other organizations, such as the PAC, now have to make this choice.

"The very stage of negotiation towards a new constitution which we have reached here at CODESA, now makes it imperative that the ANC and others who wish to participate will have to terminate armed struggle before such participants can really enter into binding, legitimate, reliable, and credible peaceful agreements."

In his now familiar manner, Mohamed allowed Mandela to respond, even though the ANC had already taken its turn. Mandela launched into an attack in front of the media. The attack effectively destroyed de Klerk. He will never recover. This is what Mandela said:

"Thank you, Mr. Chairman. I said I would like to raise a matter of national importance, and I am happy you have given me the opportunity to do so. I am gravely concerned about the behaviour of Mr. de Klerk today. He has launched an attack on the African National Congress, and in doing so he has been less than frank. Even the head of an illegitimate, discredited, minority regime as his, has certain moral standards to uphold. He has no excuse, because he is a representative of a discredited regime, not to uphold moral standards. He has handled — and before I say so, let me say that no wonder the Conservative Party has made such a serious inroad to his power base. You understand why.

"If a man can come to a conference of this nature and play the type of politics which are contained in his paper, very few people would like to deal with such a man. We have handled the question of Umkhonto WeSizwe in a constructive manner. We pointed out that this is one of the issues we are discussing with the Government. We had bilateral discussions but in his paper, although I was with him, I was discussing with him until about 20h20 [8:20 PM] last night, he never even hinted that he was going to make this attack. The members of the Government persuaded us to allow them to speak last. They were very keen to say the last word here. It is now clear why they did so. And he has abused his position because he hoped that I would not reply. He was completely mistaken. I am replying now. We are still prepared to have discussions with him if he wants, but he must forget that he can impose conditions on the African National Congress and, I daresay, on any one of the political organizations here.

"I have tried very hard, in discussions with him, that firstly his weakness is to look at matters from the point of view of the National Party and the white minority in this country, not from the point of view of the population of South Africa. I have gone further to say to him, no useful purpose will be served by the ANC trying to undermine the National Party, because we wanted the National Party to carry the whites in this initiative. And I have said to him on countless occasions that no useful purpose will be served by the National Party trying to undermine the African National Congress. He continues to do exactly that and we are going to stop him.

"He has told you — and I say he is less than frank, because he has not told you that it is the African National Congress, not the National Party, nor his Government that started this initiative. I have been discussing with Mr. Kobie Coetsee and other top Government officials since July 1986, when I was still in prison, asking the ANC and the Government should [sic] sit down to explore a peaceful solution. As a result of the pressure of the people inside this country and of the international community, and as a result of persuasion from us, they eventually agreed to sit sown to discuss with us. We have gone a long way in trying to contribute to the creation of an atmosphere whereby this initiative can succeed. As part of that effort, we suspended the armed struggle. What has happened on the side of the Government? We suspended the armed struggle in spite of the fact that our people were being killed and the Government, with all its capacity to put an end to the violence, were doing nothing to stop the slaughter of innocent people.

"I have said to him: You have got a strong, well-equipped, efficient Police Force and Defense Force. Why are you not using that capacity to stop this violence? I have pointed out to him that the perception that exists amongst our people is that in the forefront of this violence, are elements of the Security Forces. No doubt. It is common knowledge that organisations like the CCB, their main task is to eliminate freedom fighters in this country. So many activists have been killed, without trace. The killers have never been traced, or hardly ever traced. And in those massacres not a single member of the National Party was even grazed with a spear. It is all activists who are in your position who fight apartheid.

"Nevertheless, we have told him, and done things to show our commitment to the peace process. I have indicated that only last night I had a discussion with him about this very Declaration of Intent. There were certain loopholes which, when it was reported to us, we found in the document, and I was instructed to ensure that those loopholes are closed. I discussed the matter with him. He then persuaded me, saying that this document has gone through to the relevant committees. We must not amend it at this moment. I agreed with him. And I went back to the committee to say, it is now too late for us to do anything. They accepted that because of our commitment to the peace process, our desire that this process should succeed. Now he is attacking us because we have not dissolved Umkhonto. He is not even telling you, reporting to you that when we agreed, we had a discussion in Cape Town at the beginning of this year on Umkhonto WeSizwe. We then had an agreement in terms of which we had to hand over our weapons for joint control by the Government and ourselves, but we linked that to the development of the political process.

"We said when the process has reached a certain stage, which can ensure that we would have an effective control or say in Government, then it would be easy because that would be our Government. Their army will be our army. We would be ready at that time to do so. That was the spirit of our discussions and I have met him — I have met him for example before the signing of the Peace Accord, when he was threatening to do then what he has done now — and I say to him: You are asking us to do something. You are asking us to commit suicide, because when your Government is not prepared to intervene and stop the violence; when the perception amongst our people is that it is elements in the Security Forces that are killing our people; when our people are demanding to be armed, what political organisation would hand over its weapons to the same man who is regarded by the people as killing innocent people.

"And I asked him not to insist on this because we would never agree, and I told him that we should discuss the matter and see whether we can reach a solution. And I met him Thursday, last week. He raised the same point. I again emphasized to him that he is asking us to do something that is absolutely ridiculous and that we wouldn't do so. We could never give our arms to a

Government which we are sure either has lost control over the Security Forces or the Security Forces are doing precisely what he wants them to do. I can't see any head of Government who would allow such a culture of violence to take root, without interfering. We have discussed certain mechanisms and agreed that these mechanisms should be applied, in documents setting out the principles of the Peace Accord.

"Nevertheless, in spite of these mechanisms, violence still continues in this country and he has given a lot of statistics to show how many new policemen have been employed, what courts have been created. He does not relate what is happening, because in spite of what he has done, the incidence of violence is growing, is increasing in the country. And I regret very much that he should try to take advantage of this meeting for petty, political gains. It confirms what we have been saying all along, that the National Party and the government have a double agenda. They are talking peace to us. They are at the same time conducting a war. They are busy doing certain things which are unacceptable, using taxpayers' money. They are funding certain organisations through the Police and he comes forward and says he didn't know about it. If the head of the Government does not know when as much as R7 million is spent, he doesn't know about it, then he is not fit to be a head of a government.

"He is calling on us to disband Umkhonto WeSizwe, yet hit squads are operating freely in this country. When we heard that at the funeral of a prominent activist, Sam Ntuli, who was gunned down by the same hit squads, as the mourners were dispersing, eighteen people were killed in broad daylight and the Police were in the vicinity. It was clear that these were killers who were carrying out their job in the knowledge that the law enforcement agencies would not interfere with them. They walked away freely, without fear of any detection. You can make your own inferences at that.

"If Mr. de Klerk promises to do his duty as the head of Government, to put an end to the violence, to restrain his security services, to clean the country of hit squads and other elements which are responsible for killing innocent people, then he can come to us and say: I want you to hand over your weapons to us for joint control. But as long as he's playing this double game, he must be clear that we are not going to co-operate with him on this matter. He can do what he likes. We are not going to disband Umkhonto WeSizwe. We are not a political party. We are a political organisation, perhaps with more support worldwide than he has. We have used Umkhonto WeSizwe to help in the exertion of pressure on the Government to change its policies.

"We have no illusions. It is not the operations of Umkhonto alone which have brought about these developments, but Umkhonto has had a very significant contribution towards the struggle and we cannot hand over that instrument to the National Party. I must appeal to him to work harmoniously and seriously with the African National Congress. This is our initiative. A number of people have paid him compliments. Very well, we agree with that. He has tried to undo what his brothers have done to us. Through the policy of apartheid, we have created misery beyond words. Nevertheless, we are prepared to forget and say he has made a contribution towards normalizing the situation because without him we would not have made this progress. I ask him to place his cards on the table face upwards. Let's work together, openly. Let there be no secret agendas. Let him not persuade us that he should be the last speaker because he wants to abuse the privilege and to attack us in the hope that he will get no reply.

"I am prepared to work with him in spite of all his mistakes. And I am prepared to make allowances because he is a product of apartheid. Although he wants these democratic changes, he has sometimes very little idea what democracy means and his statement here, many people will regard it as very harsh, where he is threatening us, where he says this cannot be done. He is forgetting that he cannot speak like a representative of a

Government which has got legitimacy and which represents the majority of the population.

"These are statements which can only be used by somebody who represents the majority of the population in the country. He doesn't represent us. He can't talk to us in that language, but nevertheless I am prepared to work with him to see to it that these democratic changes are introduced in the country and we can only succeed if we are candid and open with one another. This type of thing, of trying to take advantage of the co-operation which we are giving him willingly, is something extremely dangerous and I hope this is the last time he will do so.

"Thank you very much, Mr. Chairman."

Apart from the many obvious contradictions, the speech was grandstanding at its best. The president of the communist-led ANC sounded like a madman. Too many of his words meant nothing.

The Failure of CODESA

Instead of giving Mandela and his communist terrorists a strong warning about the consequences of not disbanding MK, de Klerk sheepishly tried to defend himself and in effect apologized to Mandela. He has never recovered and never will. For all practical purposes, de Klerk now has to dance to the ANC's tune.

Mandela's tantrum raises many troubling questions. More important, it reveals why the communists fail to honor their signed agreements. Conveniently, if the ANC considers the present South African government "discredited and illegitimate" it cannot honor any agreements made with it. Agreements which involve "illegitimate" parties can never be binding. The ANC/SACP wants only one thing: the total transfer of power from the present government to itself.

When this was not achieved at CODESA II in May 1992, the ANC/SACP and allied parties walked out of the talks and embarked on "mass action" which was designed to topple the present government before the end of 1992, a pipe dream. The ANC/SACP cannot topple any government. They tried it in Bophuthatswana and failed; they tried it in Ciskei and failed; and they tried it in KwaZulu and failed dismally. But, like all terrorists, they have not learned that terror and intimidation always fail.

The lack of a democratic tradition in South Africa means that people there have no concept of how a democratic process works. Too many of those involved in the negotiations believe that democracy can be achieved overnight, once and for all. They are unaware of the long, drawn-out process which yields results in stages, and sometimes in small doses.

When the ANC walked out of the talks, its Secretary General, Cyril Ramaphosa, from Venda, one of MK's strongholds, announced that "nothing" had been achieved in the negotiations and time had been wasted. Yet, four out of five CODESA working groups reached agreement. In reality, CODESA produced 80 percent agreement and, even the remaining twenty percent could have been negotiated. Ramaphosa's wild distortion of CODESA shows the extent to which his organization, the ANC and allies are married to dictatorship. In exile, the ANC/SACP operated as a totalitarian entity. They know nothing else. They kill anyone who questions their course. Camps were established so they could torture and murder anyone who raised questions.

It was clear at CODESA that the communist-led ANC had not abandoned its goal to seize power. Inside South Africa, the organization was steadily losing much of whatever credibility it had. There were signs of this development on the international scene as well. When people heard Mandela call for sanctions in 1992, they believed he is well along the road to senility.

One of the best outcomes of CODESA was the distinct emergence of two power blocks: the Stalinists and the Democrats. Ten parties formed the Stalinist Alliance. They included the ANC/SACP; Natal Indian Congress/Transvaal

Indian Congress; the Colored Labour Party, Transkei and others. Most of them were intimidated by the communists. At CODESA I and II, Inkatha Freedom Party, Ciskei, Bophuthatswana, and others vigorously opposed the communists. This development meant that the people of South Africa will have a clear choice between the tyranny of obsolete Stalinism and the freedom which only democracy can guarantee.

On the surface, CODESA may have seemed such a good beginning that too many people expected final results. This could not be. CODESA had too many flaws. It was not inclusive enough nor was it ever quite clear what was being negotiated. The group was elitist and the "people" were completely shut out. Now that the lines are clear, the process should be opened to other groups. The future of South Africa cannot be negotiated by politicians alone.

Of all the races in South Africa, blacks — excluding coloreds and Indians — should be the ones most anxious to get real talks going. Delays will affect them most adversely. The idea of "black majority rule" is a dangerous myth. Unprepared blacks, on their own, or even as a majority in government, cannot govern South Africa. The result would be worse than anything we have seen in the disastrous rest of black Africa. One has only to look at what happened in exile where the ANC had power. The present anarchy in black townships where the communists are in control demonstrates what would happen in South Africa under a communist-led ANC government.

To insist that blacks alone can govern South Africa immediately is to deny the devastating effects of apartheid which, among other things, denied blacks the proper education, training, and experience needed to run a modern state efficiently and effectively. Mere education and training are not enough. Kwame Nkrumah held degrees from American universities. As president, he ruined Ghana. Julius Nyerere had a degree from Great Britain. He ruined his country, Tanzania.

Agastino Neto had degrees from Portugal. He ruined Angola. Robert Mugabe has degrees from South Africa and also earned a string of degrees by correspondence while he was in prison. He continues to ruin Zimbabwe. In fact, Mugabe's case is most pathetic. Not only is he an intelligent man, he inherited a strong economy from Ian Smith and, at one time, probably had the best educated cabinet in black Africa, yet Zimbabwe today, after twelve years of majority rule, is a basket case. Mugabe should have appointed Ian Smith as Minister of Development in the President's Office. Smith, who was well-connected internationally, could have attracted investments to Zimbabwe. By being in the President's Office, Smith would have gained prestige, Mugabe would have been able to watch him, and the country would have prospered. Experience in governing and shared leadership are the missing pieces across Africa. "Independence" has somehow pre-empted transition.

During a 30-year period when the Stalinist ANC/SACP leadership was in exile, over half a billion dollars was raised by the ANC communists in the name of "suffering black South Africans" who needed to be "liberated." A "government-in-waiting," as the Stalinists refer to themselves, could have educated and trained thousands of accountants, bankers, doctors, lawyers, engineers, teachers, scientists, social workers, administrators, diplomats, pilots, managers, civil servants, policemen, the people who would make the country governable. Instead, millions of black minds went to waste as black school children heeded the call of the ANC/SACP to "choose liberation before education" and dropped out of school, burned down schools, libraries and laboratories, beat up and murdered teachers, set up "peoples' courts" and sentenced adults to public flogging and death. Young boys raped their own mothers in the name of "liberation." This is the costly legacy of the ANC government-in-exile: 30 wasted years.

The communist-led ANC leadership will abandon the millions who are in townships and who are being used by the Stalinists to ruin South Africa. Already the leadership is moving out of townships into the plush suburbs of Johannesburg. Places like Soweto and others will become cesspools of poverty, violence, and crime and the residents will be ravaged by AIDS and other diseases. Those who presently dance in the streets in praise of Mandela, Slovo, Ramaphosa, and Jay Naidoo will be abandoned by these their "leaders" in time. The magnitude of the tragedy awaiting millions of black South Africans, which is the result of the criminal actions of the communist-led ANC leadership, in the words of a former South African President, "is too ghastly to contemplate."

The Political Condition of South African Blacks

To govern a modern state includes managing the resources — natural, human, created, and spiritual — of a country in such a way that every citizen has a fair and equal chance of success. For this to happen, expertise is indispensable. There must be people in sufficient numbers who can keep the water supply running; electricity transmission functioning; the financial institutions working; health services accessible; the lines of communication open; transportation working; and food supplies and shelter at adequate levels. The educational system must be relevant and available to all. The citizens must be protected and must have stability and peace.

All these functions, and many more, require educated, trained, and experienced personnel. South Africa does not now have enough trained and experienced blacks to run Johannesburg effectively, let alone the whole country of South Africa. The ANC cannot even run its own headquarters in Johannesburg. Inefficiency, incompetence, corruption, and nepotism abound. Transkei, the first black state in South Africa to declare its independence, is a total disaster. In less than twenty years of independence, the country has had two military coups and is presently run by a corrupt military junta whose dictator, General Holomisa, lectured delegates to CODESA on democracy. Everything that happened in black

Africa in the last thirty years can happen in black South Africa. The clear signs are already there.

Majority rule in South Africa, as opposed to mob rule, is hardly worth discussing. With millions of blacks 35 years of age and younger uneducated, unemployable, undisciplined, and violent — the so-called "lost generation" — effective participation in government is inconceivable. Unless something drastic is done, the "lost generation" and possibly their children too, will be at best the "hewers of wood and drawers of water" in the new South Africa. They will have the vote probably only once, by virtue of age, but they will never experience real freedom of choice.

Before actual democracy begins to emerge in South Africa, certain painful realities will have to be addressed. South Africa, at this time, is two major worlds and one minor one; a kind of uneasy trinity. There is the Euroculture World, the Afroculture World, and the Nonculture World. The Euroculture World is the world of opinion polls; European customs and traditions; campaigns; elections; Christianity; secret ballots and democracy. The Afroculture World is a world of African custom and traditions; hereditary leadership; supremacy of elders; extended families; African traditional religions and ancestors. The Nonculture World is the world of chaos, anarchy, violence, crime — the township and squatter camps.

There are huge gaps among the world views, the understanding and interpretation of reality and the values of the peoples who occupy these worlds. The Euroculture World is the dominant world and will be for a long time to come. Intellectually, this is not difficult to understand. Emotionally, it is very hard to accept. However, on closer examination, the traditional value systems of the Euroculture and Afroculture worlds are not in conflict. The real conflict is between the Euroculture world and the Nonculture World on the one hand and the Afroculture World and the Nonculture World on the other. The Nonculture World is the universal stumbling block.

If progress towards democracy in South Africa is to be made, careful thought has to be given to the question of how to move the Afroculture World toward the success of the Euroculture World without destroying Afroculture roots. How, for example, does a particular community move from a hereditary leadership to an elected leadership in a democratic way? This is not as simple as it may appear, because it is tied to emotions, attitudes, customs, history, and traditions. These are more difficult to change than laws.

The Nonculture World is the single greatest impediment to a new South Africa and, because of its cancerous characteristics, it demands concerted and immediate attention.

Chapter 10

The Lost Generation
Where the ANC Road Leads:

A nation that corrupts its youth marches to slavery.

I was born into an extended family in which there were many grown-up people I could turn to for support — uncles, aunts, grandparents, and parents. There were also many children, including cousins and siblings. This family network provided me with guidance, advice, care, and love.

I was also taught discipline and, above all, to respect especially all those who were older than I was, regardless of who they were.

By the time I entered school, at age six, I already knew very well the difference between good and bad behavior. I did not always behave well at school. When I did misbehave I was punished by my teachers. I learned very quickly never to mention to my parents that I had been punished at school because they too would punish me. The conventional wisdom at the time was that teachers were always right and whoever was punished at school deserved it. To deserve punishment, however, was considered a disgrace by the family. Hence, further punishment at home.

In addition to my home and school, the community in which we as a family lived, and the church, contributed significantly to my upbringing. Even with all this support and education or molding, I did not always live up to expectations. Peer pressure and my own rebellious nature sometimes led me astray. As an adult, I shudder when I think of what could have happened to me if I had been left to my own devices at a tender age. Even worse things could have happened if I had been led astray by adults systematically teaching me to hate, be violent, use drugs, disrespect my own parents, teachers, the law, the clergy, and others in positions of authority. I often wonder what would have happened to me and my siblings if we had been taught that life was worth nothing and that killing for political reasons was an heroic act.

Any right-thinking person is bound to say: "No child can be taught such evil." It happened in South Africa. The results are devastating. Millions of relatively young, black South Africans now aged between six and thirty make up the "Lost Generation." They are functionally illiterate, unemployable, undisciplined, and menacingly violent. They have been so dehumanized that they act like monsters. They are victims of a premeditated and systematically executed program to enslave black South Africans for generations.

Teaching Anarchy to Children

It all started in 1976. That year, thousands of black students took to the streets in several townships. Their aim was to demonstrate peacefully against an inferior system of education which was forced on them by the apartheid regime. Their actions were no different from what students in any democratic country would have done.

South Africa's political tradition is one of brute force. The country was founded through force and for more than three centuries has been sustained through force.

Even though the students acted on their own, the South African government resorted to lies and blamed the demonstrations on communist agitators. The police and army were then given orders to shoot. These actions of the police and army contrasted sharply with those of the German police and army during my student days there. When we demonstrated, the police turned on their water canons and we were all drenched. No one was shot or seriously injured.

As news of the student deaths was broadcast around the world, the ANC-in-exile issued statements claiming that they had organized the student demonstrations. Student leaders in South Africa refuted this claim especially because many of them identified with the Black Consciousness Movement and not with the ANC.

However, because the ANC had camps in various African countries and the Black Consciousness Movement had none, most of the students who escaped from South Africa found their way to the ANC camps. It was a question of survival. The students were promised scholarships which would enable them to study abroad or, for those who so chose, military training and other opportunities. The reality is that most of them either died fighting foreign wars in Zimbabwe, Ethiopia, and Angola, or were murdered by the ANC in Angola, Zambia, Uganda, and Tanzania, or just wasted in these countries. Only a handful ever saw the inside of an academic institution.

In 1977, while the memory of the 1976 massacre was still fresh in the minds of black students and parents in South Africa, the ANC issued a call from the safety of its headquarters in Lusaka, Zambia. The students in South Africa were told to "choose liberation before education." It was a deadly blow from which millions of black South Africans will never recover. The ANC leaders who advocated this form of mental and spiritual genocide did not follow their own advice. They sent their own children to the best schools overseas. Mandela's daughter, who studied in Boston, received a scholarship which enabled her to fly to Switzerland regularly on skiing trips. Tutu sent his children to America and England. One daughter, who had no qualifications to study medicine, was nevertheless given a medical scholarship at Emory University. Tens of thousands of dollars were wasted on tutoring her so she could keep up. Yet when two highly qualified black teachers sought scholarships to study education at the Masters level, they were denied on the grounds that Emory had no funds. The real reason is that they are not Tutu's children.

All the leaders of the ANC plant their children in the most expensive private schools while they tell the children of the poor not to go to school. Chris Hani, the slain Communist Party General Secretary, sent his daughter to one of the most expensive private schools in South Africa. Until his death, he had never held a job.

The angry, highly politicized students dropped out of school and began their long march to slavery. They burned down schools, libraries, and laboratories. Those students who still wanted to go to school were forcibly prevented. Teachers were beaten, stabbed, shot, and murdered by students. In most of the black townships a climate in which education could take place was replaced by chaos.

Things predictably went from bad to worse when students associated themselves with different political parties and then formed rival student political groups on campuses. Parents did the same. By 1980, the seeds of disaster had firmly taken root in most black township schools.

The ANC sent young inexperienced children from bases in Angola, Zambia, and Tanzania to South Africa on suicide missions. No preparations for guerrilla warfare had been made inside South Africa. Most of the youths were arrested on arrival by the security police, tried for terrorism, found guilty, and sentenced to death. When that happened, ANC leaders-in-exile would go to the United Nations, the Queen of England, and the Pope to implore them to rush to the Pretoria regime, to ask for clemency and mercy. More often than not the youth were sent to the gallows. The young martyrs went, heads high, declaring for all the world to hear: "Let our blood nourish the trees that will bear the fruits of freedom." Even though the young guerrillas showed remarkable courage, it was clear they were being used. They did not and could not understand the treachery associated with power politics.

They were sacrificed to a non-existent armed struggle. Clearly blacks were not running this futile exercise. White and Indian communists were. Black leaders in the so-called armed wing of the ANC were mere stooges.

By 1984, the ANC leadership living in luxury in Zambia and London, called on the black youth inside South Africa to "make South Africa ungovernable." Through radio broadcasts from Lusaka and Ethiopia, the black youth were told the ANC was engaged in a struggle "to overthrow the Pretoria regime and to seize power." The young blacks were told to kill all those who were not part of the armed struggle since they were "puppets" and not fit to live.

Time magazine acknowledged this situation in 1991:

> "He says to call him 'Che Guevara'.... At 22 he is a hardened veteran of the struggle against apartheid. He has killed 'enemies of the people' and is prepared to kill again.
>
> "Seven years ago he became a supporter of the then outlawed African National Congress. With other teenagers he started stoning police vehicles. When leaders of the liberation movement sought to make the townships ungovernable, he became one of the enforcers. If he caught a family paying rent to municipal authorities in defiance of the rent boycott, he would serve them with an eviction notice. 'If they refused to go,' he says, 'we'd speak to them in the language of the struggle. We'd kill them and burn their house down.'" (February 18, 1991)

In 1986, Winnie Mandela told the young that they would liberate South Africa with matches and tires. This is the savage practice of burning human beings alive after they have been found guilty by peoples' courts. The victims are those accused of collaborating with the apartheid regime. The previously quoted *Time* article detailed this ANC practice:

> "Thousands upon thousands of others are tough political activists. They seem to roam the townships like so many deputy sheriffs, setting down the law of the

street and enforcing it with harsh punishment.... teenage judges presided over so-called people's courts that almost casually handed out death sentences to suspected traitors. A youth invention that has not disappeared is 'necklacing,' the method of mob-execution in which a gasoline-doused rubber tire is thrown around a suspected traitor's body and set ablaze."

Burning human beings is barbaric beyond description and must be condemned in no uncertain terms. To call the practice "necklacing" is an abomination because in traditional culture of black South Africa a necklace is a symbol of love. The practice is unworthy of those who claim to be fighting oppression and disqualifies them from membership in any civilized society.

It is significant too, that members of the Black Consciousness Movement were the main target. This is the organization which was founded by Steve Biko. It emphasized black pride and self reliance and had a substantial following among the youth. The white and Indian communists saw this movement as a dangerous threat to their plans of creating a communist state in South Africa. Hence, the two-pronged approach of getting the youth out of school and burning the leadership of the Black Consciousness Movement. If Steve Biko had not been brutally murdered by the South African police, there would be no "Lost Generation." The communists also targeted for burning members of AZAPO, PAC, and Inkatha.

Installing a Communist Agenda

But, it must be stressed that the white and Indian communists inflicted the greatest and most lasting damage on the black youth. In contrast to the youth of the other population groups, black youth were systematically trained by the communists to be anarchists and murderers. They were trained to "make South Africa ungovernable" by implementing the following program:

- Use intimidation, force, terror, and fear on a wide scale, even against their own parents and relatives.

- Kill and terrorize black elected officials and their families. Councilors who are in charge of black townships are prime targets.
- Provoke violent action to cause the authorities to act with determination to restore order; then accuse them of violence. Call for the removal of the police. When this is done, accuse the government of not maintaining order. Declare a "breakdown in law and order."
- Politicize all aspects of life, especially education, in the name of the struggle. Use every possible sector to promote the revolutionary program.
- Pretend to promote "reconciliation" while simultaneously stimulating and provoking social unrest and mass demonstrations. At the same time blame others for sowing social strife.
- Create hostility towards the police.
- Create a profound "guilt complex" in clerics, trendy politicians, academics, and liberal leaders.
- Defame those who try to point out the dangers of abandoning school.
- Ridicule all loyal, patriotic citizens and organizations.
- Stimulate racial hatred, divisions, fear, and prejudice between whites and blacks and between the various black groups.
- Mobilize and manipulate South Africa's black workers.
- Speak in symbolic terms and always call for "freedom."
- Conquer the student mind. Use student riots to foment public protest.
- Infiltrate cadres and fellow travelers into the schools, universities, and technical schools. Grab control of teacher's organizations, student newspapers, and youth groups.
- Always delegitimize the government by terming it "the regime."
- Discredit and attack the security forces on all occasions.
- Set up your own "self-defense units." Demand active participation by all the community's doctors, communications

people, home-made weapons manufacturers, and even small children.
- Discredit or assassinate those who try to obstruct you.
- Identify civil servants, journalists, and politicians who may be vulnerable to control through intimidation or blackmail.
- Discredit Western/Christian culture by degrading all forms of artistic expression: theater, art films, literature.
- Corrupt other young people. Get them away from religion. Get them interested in sex, drugs, pornography.
- Discredit the family as an institution. Break down the parent/child relationship.
- "Always preach democracy, but seize power as fast and as ruthlessly as possible." (Lenin)
- Maintain the pressure on all sides till people are thoroughly weary and in despair and will surrender to any false promise — "anything for the sake of peace."

(Adapted from: *What A Marxist South Africa Would Mean To You*. Aida Parker, Johannesburg, 1992. pp. 29 - 31.)

This program has led to an unprecedented level of fear in the black townships. One of the tactics the ANC uses is to call for a rent boycott in the townships. When this happens, no one is allowed to pay rent to the authorities. At that point many honest, hard-working people want to pay their rent but are afraid to, because they might be burned out or killed as threatened by "Che Guevara."

At one time, these boycotts forced the Transvaal Provincial Administration (South Africa's Housing Authority) to consider writing off $350 million in unpaid rent, according to the Johannesburg newspaper *The Star* (July 13, 1990). So many people weren't paying (41 percent in Soweto), the government thought they would have to write the money off and get it from the taxpayers.

Through such actions on the part of the ANC, the youth are being taught that anarchy pays.

After Mandela was released in 1990 and the ANC unbanned, young blacks were further victimized in 1990 when they were told by the ANC that they had nothing to worry about since a communist government would nationalize the mines, the banks, and key industries along with redistributing the wealth. Their future was bright.

The Dehumanized Youth

After more than a decade of being trained as anarchists, a large percentage of South Africa's black youth cannot behave like normal human beings. They do not know what this means. They were taught only violence.

This violence is by and large directed at blacks who refuse to tow the communist-led ANC line. The youth conduct peoples' courts in the townships where children as young as ten years old put adults on "trial" and mete out sentences which can range from public floggings to death by burning. Township communities are terrorized and forced to join the ANC. Then the liberal media in South Africa and abroad claim that the ANC has the largest black following in South Africa.

How can people support an organization which has dehumanized and destroyed their children? How can they support any organization which teaches young children to use drugs, to steal, to hate, terrorize, rape, torture, plunder, and murder? How can sensible, intelligent people vote for an organization which has turned a whole generation into sub-humans?

Even though the terrorized residents of the townships are ignored by the media, they understand what is going on. They know that whites and Indians direct the activities of the ANC. They know that mandrax, a crack-like drug, is smuggled into South Africa from India. The white and Indian communists supply this drug to black children in the townships. The kids use it and go on the rampage. They have been known to burn down black-owned businesses, so that blacks will be forced to patronize Indian-owned businesses.

These youngsters are the backbone of the ANC "mass action" campaign. Mass action is actually mass intimidation. Blacks are forced to participate in strikes, boycotts, and stayaways. Like the Nazi storm troopers, black youths in South African townships have unleashed a reign of terror hitherto unknown there. Even under the darkest and most brutal days of apartheid, blacks in the townships and squatter camps never lived in such terror as they do now. Parents live in constant fear of their own children. Thousands of blacks have died in these townships since Mandela's release three years ago. In fact, more blacks have died since Mandela's release than at any other period in South African history. Yet the liberal media anoint him the leader of all black South Africans and claim that he is destined to be the first black president of the new South Africa. The same media have never credited blacks with any appreciable degree of intelligence.

The people who have sold their souls are those blacks in the communist-led ANC, including Nelson Mandela. He has been a slave of his white and Indian communist masters since the 1950s. How these blacks can be part of schemes which are designed to destroy their own youth is evidence of the power of communism. Joseph Stalin murdered millions of his own people. Mao Tse Tung did the same. Mandela publicly praises both murderers as "the greatest men in history." He obviously aspires to be like them.

The "Lost Generation" do not want negotiations. They want to fight. Many of them now realize that if negotiations succeed, they will be the biggest losers. Their votes will only serve to put white and Indian communists into power. Once communists have the power they will turn around and slaughter the unruly youth. The Lost Generation know that without education and skills they are doomed to be "hewers of wood and drawers of water" for as long as they live. The communists who manipulate them will forget them and they will perish in abject poverty. The greatest number of AIDS victims will also come from them and their children. They are right in thinking this way. When all the vestiges of apartheid have been removed, the "Lost Generation" will become the biggest losers in victory.

Many in the "Lost Generation" camp have openly rebelled against the aging men in the ANC. They realize now that the organization that was supposed to liberate them is not just white and Indian-led, but is "rotten" and "hollow." Panic has set in among the ranks of the elite communists. In an effort to placate the "Lost Generation," after they publicly booed him and walked out of the Soweto stadium, Mandela promised them guns. This man, who wants to arm children with lethal weapons, is supposed to become the president of a new South Africa, according to the liberals. More than 80 percent of the deaths in South Africa are caused by guns, especially Russian-made AK-47's, the ANC's weapon of choice. How can any responsible adult promise guns to 12-year-olds? The man who is supposedly the "hope of the future" is demonstrably a criminal. To intentionally destroy the futures of millions of young people is criminal. Dictators always abuse children, forcing them to do their dirty work.

As if that were not enough, in May 1993, Mandela demanded that the voting age be lowered to 14 in South Africa. He knows that black adults will not vote for the ANC because it is led by communists. This means that in a ANC government, whites and Indians will have the real power, hence the support from liberals. Since communism is infinitely far worse than apartheid, any hopes of freedom blacks have in South Africa will be dashed. Blacks will be enslaved - mentally, spiritually and physically. That is what happened in the former Soviet Union, and Eastern Europe. That is what is happening in China and Cuba. Fourteen-year-olds cannot understand this. To their immature minds, Marxist slogans are in fact attainable goals. I thought so too, until I went to study in Czechoslovakia in 1963. That is when I discovered that communism is not just worse than apartheid; it is a thoroughly evil system. Mandela's call to allow 14-year-olds to vote reveals his political vulnerability.

South Africa's Great Challenge

The greatest challenge facing all black South Africans — regardless of political or other affiliations — is how to breathe life into millions of young black South Africans whose emotions and brains have been virtually destroyed by the communists. These are our children and grandchildren. This is our shame as black people. Without them, the future for blacks after apartheid will be bleak. They represent lost opportunities. They could have been — perhaps some can still be — doctors, engineers, scientists, artists, teachers, nurses, administrators, leaders, and social workers. They represent what it takes to govern a country. The real intention of the white and Indian communists was to make sure that black youth were so systematically deformed that they will be unfit to govern. The target was never apartheid. The target was the black race. Not just a grave injustice, but enormous damage with far-reaching consequences has been done.

I do not believe that all is lost. The "Lost Generation" can still be found; it can and must be rehabilitated. We do not have to reinvent the wheel. Through specially designed educational and training programs which include a rehabilitation component, millions of young, lost, black South African youth can be rescued and given a second chance. A new constitution with all its fancy provisions cannot save the "Lost Generation." Even if the Angels write the constitution and hand it to us, the "Lost Generation" will tear it up.

If the problem of the "Lost Generation" is to be addressed effectively, the following two steps must be taken:

1. Education must be depoliticized. Education is a basic human right and, therefore, must be above party politics.
2. The highly politicized and divisive parent and student groups must disband and schools should once again become what they

were intended to be: places for teaching, learning, fun, and growth.

For the sake of the lost black children of South Africa, black adults must bury their petty differences and take appropriate steps to save the black youth. This is a challenge far greater than what apartheid posed. Only blacks themselves can do this. It is our responsibility. No one else's purposes are served by saving the blacks. Abdication of this responsibility by blacks invites slavery.

Chapter 11

Which Road To Follow?

After living in exile for 29 years I look back and conclude that to me apartheid was a curse and a blessing. It was a curse because I was forced to leave home, family, friends, and the country I love. I wish I could have spent more time with my parents, especially my grandfather, a man of great wisdom and humility. I could have learned so much more from him. But, it does not help to cry over spilled milk.

Exile was good to me too. I have lived in eight different countries and I have seen most of the world, including much of black Africa. Whenever I think of the future of South Africa I cannot help feeling pessimistic because of what I have seen in most of black Africa.

Africa is a continent of great paradoxes and contradictions. In natural resources it is the world's richest continent and, as such, has most of the requirements for economic development and prosperity. Yet it is the most impoverished continent and is saddled with political chaos, economic and social disintegration, ignorance, disease, and wars. Half the world's refugees are in Africa and it is predicted that in a few years Africa will lead the world in AIDS cases and deaths. As we approach the 21st century, Africans may be offended when they hear that theirs is a "dark continent." What we cannot deny is that Africa, despite her beautiful sunshine, is a continent wallowing in deep darkness, and has no sense of direction economically, politically, socially, and, above all, spiritually. When one considers that Liberia and Ethiopia, which have been black-ruled for over one hundred years and yet now stand in virtual ruin because of senseless wars, one has little ground for optimism.

Africa's Guilt

It is fashionable to blame colonialism for all the ills of Africa. There are some, particularly Western, apologists who claim that Africa needs massive foreign aid in order for her to be rescued and started on the road to economic development, political stability, peace, and prosperity.

In the years since Ghana became independent in 1957, billions of dollars in the form of grants, loans, and investments have been poured into Africa, mainly by Western nations. There is precious little to show for the efforts. More money is clearly not the answer. At the root of Africa's woes is insatiable greed on the part of most African leaders. Unless a new and honest leadership emerges, black African countries are doomed. Like the legendary African empires of old, modern day Africa will be reduced to ruins.

There is no doubt in my mind that if the ANC comes to power in South Africa, the end of civilization in all of black Africa will become a reality. There is, however, a viable alternative to the ANC's plans for South Africa — an alternative which will bring real freedom to the peoples of South Africa and hope to the rest of black Africa.

Mention has been made of the fact that South Africa is, like the former Soviet Union, a colonial creation which was maintained by brutal force against the will of the majority; hence its failure after 300 years of existence. It follows that if a lasting solution has to be found, that solution must be based on the will of the peoples of South Africa — not just the politicians. What the different peoples of South Africa must decide is how they are going to relate to one another in the post-apartheid era.

Undoing the Past

At the center of South Africa's problems is the question of the land which blacks lost through conquest. How much of that land must be returned to the indigenous peoples? This is a complex problem, as the ongoing court battles between American Indians and different U.S. states reveals. In America, the Indians are a small minority and are at the mercy of the courts. In South Africa, however, the dispossessed are in the majority and at some point this will be reflected in government structures. There will be enormous pressure to confiscate land from whites and Indians and give it to blacks, as has happened in Zimbabwe. If that happens, South Africa will face a bleak future.

A strong argument can be advanced in favor of forcing the National Party government to compensate all those who were forcibly removed from their property in the last forty years. Government-owned businesses should be sold to private owners and the money used to pay the victims who were evicted from their property. This seems a fair solution.

South Africa's diversity demands a federal or confederal constitution. The idea of a government of national unity is a myth and a ploy by power-hungry politicians. Given the fact that South Africa's problems are varied and complex, it seems reasonable to go in search of regional solutions rather than attempt to solve them from a central command post. Central government in South Africa over the years has been corrupt, inefficient, wasteful, oppressive, and unresponsive to the needs of most South Africans. It is time to resort to government that is controlled by the governed.

When laying the foundation for a new South Africa, the following are some of the points that should be borne in mind:

1. Post-apartheid South Africa must evolve as a multiparty democratic state and provision must be made to rule out the possibility of a one-party state, a military coup, or any other form of dictatorship.

2. The possibility of a life-presidency must be ruled out. A life-presidency is an insult to the people. It endows an individual with qualities of deity, abilities, powers, and characteristics, while at the same time condemning the rest of the people to servitude and subhumanity. It forces a whole nation to live a lie by accepting the fallacy that only one person in the whole nation has the ability to lead. It is a transparent mask which is intended to hide the diabolism inherent in power hungriness.

3. There should be no deifying of leaders or a group of leaders. It should be remembered that the maximum price for freedom was paid by those who died in the struggle. If monuments are to be erected, they should be to their honor and memory.

4. Those elected to public office should not be allowed to form a clique that has special privileges and is above the law. Post-apartheid South Africa must develop a leadership that is humane and willing to serve rather than one which is bent on abuse of power. Special privileges such as immunity and indemnity for politicians should be completely abolished.

5. The basic, fundamental, and God-given rights of every individual will have to be safeguarded and respected. Government must carry out the wishes of the electorate and not protect the interests of a few.

6. A political career should not become a passport to ill-gotten wealth and other forms of corruption.

7. Individual and group initiative, private property, and a free-market economy must be guaranteed. Government regulation must be geared towards preventing exploitation, corruption, greed, as well as economic and political chaos. Democracy must not be restricted to "one person, one vote" but life in its totality must be democratized. Apartheid must be replaced by a system that is democratic in intent, application, and results.

8. Individual freedom must be guaranteed but national interests must be protected from destructive influences.

9. Religious freedom must be guaranteed but religious fanaticism must not be tolerated.

10. A white oligarchy must not be replaced by a black oligarchy. If post-apartheid South Africa must emerge as a viable entity, and if the full potential of the country is to be realized, freedom will have to be shared.

11. There should be limited terms of office for all elected government officials.

12. In addition to a constitutional court which is being discussed in South Africa, there should be an ethics commission at all levels of government whose functions will be to keep a watchful eye on government activity on behalf of the citizenry. This will prevent large-scale government corruption which is rampant in Africa, including South Africa.

Nowhere in the world is there real democracy. Governments throughout the world are famous for doing what they promise not to do. There was a time in England when rulers did as they pleased under the principle of the so-called "divine right of kings." In the 20th century, elected governments operate under the unspoken principle of the "divine right of politicians." In the new South Africa, this must be replaced by the "divine right of the people." Otherwise we will simply be replacing one form of dictatorship with another.

Chapter 12

The Road To Freedom

South Africa does not have to follow in the disastrous path of the rest of black Africa and disintegrate into political anarchy and economic ruin. Were that to happen, not only South Africa would be ruined, but the entire continent would follow. That must not be allowed to happen. To avert such a catastrophe, swift and decisive action must be taken.

Among the major responsibilities of any government is to protect its citizens, its borders, and its currency. I have already stated that, because of cultural diversity, South Africa needs a federal or confederatal system of government. Under such a system, the composition of the central government should reflect the country's cultural diversity and should have well-defined and restricted responsibilities. One of the functions of a central representative government will be to symbolize a future goal and hope which is the building of one nation out of the present diverse South African nations (ethnic groups). This is a critical task, one which will take several generations to accomplish.

The Role of Central Government

There are things, though, a central government can and should do. A major consideration should be the way in which the central government raises revenue. Governments do not earn money. They arbitrarily take from citizens in the form of taxes and usually waste the taxpayer's money with impunity. This procedure of taking money from hard-working citizens and wasting is what attracts criminal-minded politicians to public service and is responsible for the high level of corruption in government throughout the world. In order to avoid large-scale corruption, which any powerful central government would inherit from the present National Party government, the new central government should not have the authority to tax directly. Its revenue must come from the individual states which must have substantial input as far as how the central government spends its money.

Further, the central government should have no authority to borrow money. That should be the perogative of state governments. Both the IMF and World Bank should be kept out of South Africa while a thorough study of what these two institutions have accomplished in the rest of Africa is made. The South African economy is still the strongest in Africa, in spite of no funding from either the IMF or the World Bank.

In the area of foreign policy, the central government in the new South Africa should immediately restructure the foreign service, which is presently conducted as though we are at the beginning of the 20th century. Modern-day methods of communication make it unnecessary to maintain embassies all over the world. These days, most presidents and prime ministers are only a phone call away from one another. During the past 20 years, I have come to know many ambassadors. I am constantly amazed that they do not die from boredom. What the new South Africa will need are economic and cultural partners. These can be efficiently and productively maintained by small, well-trained staff in trade and cultural missions.

Political Obsessions

Obsession with politics in South Africa goes to preposterous lengths. Somehow too many politicians believe that they alone have answers to all of South Africa's problems. An example of this is the amount of time, energy, and resources spent arguing about such symbols as flags and anthems. If these issues were to be left to competent and impartial artists and musicians, a solution could be found in a matter of days. For example, the colors black, green, and gold are acceptable to all black South Africans. On the other hand, white, blue, and orange are acceptable to all white South Africans. In order to symbolize reconciliation, two colors should be taken from each existing flag and combined to make a new four-color flag. Black, white, orange, and green or black, white, gold, and blue should do the job.

The same can be done with the existing national anthems — *Nkosi Sikeleli Afrika* and *Die Stem*. Selecting parts from each and fusing them into one anthem is no monumental task. Each state or republic could exercise its right to chose its anthem. It should be the responsibility of the central government to guarantee the fundamental natural freedoms and responsibilities of every individual. This is important because even under a federal or confederatal system, there will always be minorities within given boundaries. Given the way human beings are, minorities can at least be ignored unless there is a mechanism guaranteeing equality before the law.

During the 20th century, Europeans burdened the world with three evil systems — communism, naziism, and apartheid. It is, therefore, imperative that the Judeo-Christian faith form the basis of the new South Africa's moral and ethical standards. There should be an ethics commission which will guarantee that these standards are maintained.

Necessary Political Principles

The new South Africa will need all the resources it can get to solve the many problems created by apartheid. Careful thought must be given to what is needed in a functional and high-efficiency government. We need to consider carefully, for example, whether in the 21st century we need a state president or head of state.

Power — the ability to make and implement decisions — is an individual and God-given right which no individual should surrender. People have a right to make decisions about various aspects of their lives. They can exercise their power to elect a government into office or to remove it from office. When they elect a government, they give it authority to manage their affairs. Unfortunately, in the 20th century, governments have abused their authority and usurped people's power. Hence the widespread corruption in governments around the world. The idea that government should do things for people is repulsive. People must do things for themselves.

The best way to keep government transparent and close to the governed is to limit both its size and authority. State government should have far greater authority and responsibilities than the central government. Each state should be responsible for its own education, health, housing, agriculture, taxation, communication, transportation, trade, commerce, energy, tourism, and police. Except for the police, all these human activities should be owned and operated privately.

The state must coordinate all these activities and protect the environment, workers, and employers. It must also pay special attention to children and women. Black children in South Africa have been badly abused by politicians. They need to be rehabilitated and helped to find their feet again. There should be no distinction between the rights and responsibilities of men and women.

Communism and apartheid in South Africa have caused enormous damage to families, epsecially black families. Without strong family units where children can be properly nurtured (educated) and instilled with values which have stood the tests of time — honesty, integrity, compassion, tolerance, and love, among others — there will not be a new South Africa. During the first few years of the new South Africa, a great deal of attention will have to be given to rehabilitating and strengthening family units.

To this must be added the need for a healthy work ethic. It is common to hear South Africans talk loosely about affirmative action. They are probably not aware that even in America, where the idea came from, affirmative action has not worked, and cannot work, no matter how good the intentions. South Africans must not attempt to copy either the American welfare system or affirmative action. The needs of the truly needy should be the responsibility of charitable organizations, not of government.

Too many politicians in South Africa speak of forming a government of national unity and of reconciliation. This is all empty talk. Politicians cannot bring about national unity since politics is by definition the art of divisiveness. It is also not in the interest of politicians to have unity since a united people will automatically diminish the power of politicians.

Reconciliation does not belong in the sphere of politics. It is a theological and spiritual concept symbolized in Christian theology by the incarnation. The Christmas hymn "Hark the Herald Angels Sing" says it well; "God and sinners reconciled." Only the devil knows what the communists in South Africa mean when they speak of reconciliation. It is dangerous to expect people whose loved ones have been slaughtered, burned to death, shot, and otherwise mutilated, to forget all this overnight and be reconciled with their murderers. Too many people in South Africa will have to go through the normal process of grieving and healing before reconciliation — not to mention unity — can take place. One has only to look at the former Yugoslavia after forty years of apparent unity. In South Africa, it will take people outside the realm of politics to facilitate the process of reconciliation, and ultimately unity.

Chapter 13

Freedom or Slavery?

The dismal failure of communism in the Soviet Union where it was born and nurtured, should provide conclusive evidence that the system is a fraud and cannot work anywhere. All talk about the possibility of South Africa becoming a communist dictatorship would seem absurd in the extreme. Yet, in South Africa, the communists claim that they will prove to the world that communism does work.

To a certain extent, black South Africans, especially the young, can be easily misled by the spurious promises of communism.

Besides South Africa's problems with the communists, she also has real trouble with the National Party government. The operative word in South Africa in 1990 was change. "Change" was generally understood to mean an end to apartheid and the beginning of a new economic, political and social order.

President de Klerk's announcement to end apartheid amounted to an admission that the system had failed. Given the present situation in South Africa, the present government should have announced that it would serve only in a caretaker capacity until the election of a democratic government could take its place. Such a caretaker administration would have taken the following steps:

1. Immediately repeal all apartheid laws.
2. Dissolve the apartheid parliament.

3. Maintain the three instruments which actually run a country — the civil service, the security branches, and the economic institutions.

4. Convene a national convention representing all sectors of South Africa's diverse population. From such a convention would emerge a body which would draft a constitution for the new South Africa.

5. Hold a national referendum to ratify the new constitution, and approve a new name for the country.

6. After the referendum, announce the date for the first national democratic election. Political parties could have then campaigned in preparation for this election, and the results of the election would have led to the formation of a new democratic government.

None of this happened. After the failure of its policies, the National Party remained in power and continued to govern as though nothing had happened. De Klerk and the National Party speak and act as though they have a mandate from the majority of South Africans. But they do not. This is the party which won an undemocratic, all-white election in 1948 by promising whites that South Africa would forever be a land of strict apartheid. It is an anomaly that an undemocratic regime without a mandate from the majority of the governed, controls the process of change and wields enormous power.

The National Party is obsessed with power and wants to maintain this at all cost.

Instead of following steps that would bring genuine democracy, President de Klerk embarked on a series of actions which were bound to lead to chaos. These are the steps he and his government took:

1. Allowed communist guerrillas to return to South Africa with their arms.

2. Failed to keep promise to insist that the communists disband their private army, Umkonto WeSizwe, when he had no intention of doing so.

3. Took no action to stop the violence unleashed by the ANC communists on unarmed black civilians.
4. Took no action when the communists refused to abide by the solemn agreements they signed.
5. Released hard-core communists, including murderers, armed robbers, and terrorists.
6. Held a series of secret talks with different political parties. Most of the talks were with the communists. This led to rumors about secret deals. The result was widespread suspicion in the country.
7. Demoralized the army and police.

The final straw came when de Klerk agreed to join the communists in "power-sharing." Their agreement calls for a government of "national unity" — which means unity between the ANC communists and the National Party. This marriage is supposed to last for five years.

Instead of de Klerk's actions resulting in the beginnings of a peaceful change to democracy, they have resulted in the following:

1. Escalating violence which has claimed the lives of thousands of innocent victims, many of them women and children.
2. A soaring crime rate. Most neighborhoods in the cities are like armed camps.
3. A proliferation of well-armed private armies.
4. Mass urbanization (a squatter crisis) has put a strain on city social services. This has produced massive squatter camps, which are characterized by poverty, disease, and despair.
5. The races are more polarized than at any other period in South African history.
6. The black youth has been radicalized. The social fabric has been torn apart.
7. ANC "mass action" has further damaged the economy.

The primary function of government is to protect its citizens, its borders, and its currency. Instead of protecting its citizens, the de Klerk government has appointed a commission, headed by Justice Richard Goldstone, who has shown a real partiality to the ANC. In his hasty pronouncements following shoddy investigations, he often sides with the communist ANC. He is clearly anti-Zulu and anti-Inkatha.

De Klerk has also invited foreigners to monitor the violence in South Africa as though it is a spectator sport, as in the days of the Roman Empire. There are teams from the United Nations (UN), the European Community (EC), and the Organization for African Unity (OAU). The violence in South Africa has to be stopped, not monitored. Neither the UN, nor the EC, nor the OAU can do that.

The UN is virtually the most hypocritical organization on earth. While it promises peace to the world, it issues edicts, such as economic embargoes, and sends troops to countries which terrorize and destroy those it says it is trying to help. The UN is a major part of world problems. It can never solve them.

The recent events in Somalia where for three nights UN soldiers slaughtered Somali women and children in their sleep is evidence of how much the UN understands about peace. It is strange that peacekeepers arrive armed to the teeth with tanks, helicopter gunships, and aircraft carriers.

If we were not dealing with matters of cruel and unnecessary destruction of human life, the presence of the OAU in South Africa would be cause for endless laughter. The OAU is nothing but what the Germans would call *Affentheater* (Theater of Apes). It is a gangster organization of murderers, thieves, and liars.

How can they monitor violence, when through their Liberation Committee they finance the training and equipping of the communist-led ANC terrorists? One has only to look at how the OAU has devastated its own countries through endless wars. Why did they not monitor violence in Ethiopia, Nigeria, and Mozambique? Why are they not now monitoring catastrophic violence in Somalia, Liberia, Sudan, Uganda, and Angola? Where were they when the Tutsi slaughtered the Hutu in Burundi, or when the Shonas in Zimbabwe slaughtered the Ndebeles soon after that country's independence in 1980?

The OAU should be made to account for the fact that half the world's population of refugees, most of them women and infants, are in Africa. They are a living testimony to Africa's violent reality. The presence of the OAU in South Africa should be recorded in the history books as the sickest and cruelest joke of all time.

What Did They Know, And When Did They Know It?

The EC is in South Africa in a vain attempt to shield itself from genuine charges of racism. Without the large sums of money which flow from the EC to the communist-led ANC the communists would not be able to finance their terrorist machinery. But it is not just the EC. Without the millions of dollars the communist-led ANC receives from Sweden, the communists would not be able to sustain the present level of violence.

There are many questions about Sweden's role in the torture and murder of young South Africans in Angola. Survivors report that the notorious MBOKODO was supplied with food from Sweden. How much did the Swedish authorities know?

The presence of the so-called international community in South Africa only makes matters worse as these organizations are there to support the communist-led ANC. There is talk that when elections are held in South Africa they should be monitored by the so-called international community. We think this would be unfair. After all, who monitors elections in the U.S., Canada, Germany, France, Israel, Britain, Australia or New Zealand? The UN "monitored" elections in Angola in 1992 and certified what was essentially a fraudulent election as "fair and free." We certainly don't need these same people involved in a South African election.

An organization which does not know what is fair and free cannot be entrusted with monitoring elections. What must happen, and happen quickly, is that all politically motivated organizations must leave South Africa. They include the UN, the EC, and the OAU.

Only one conclusion can be drawn from the foregoing: The Nationalist government has lost control and is no longer able to govern South Africa. This should come as no surprise. The National Party is an apartheid party. Without apartheid, it can have no legitimacy. The Nationalists were only able to govern through the use of brute force.

There are charges among white South Africans that de Klerk has "sold out." If he did "sell out" whites, he did so on February 2, 1990. Unfortunately for de Klerk, he did not tell whites then that the days of the National Party government were over. Three years later, he continues to mislead them by saying that there is going to be "power-sharing" — power-sharing with communists!

What has really happened is that de Klerk has been totally outmaneuvered by the communists. Since he started negotiations with them in 1990, he has steadily conceded ground to them. His own party is now in total disarray and is steadily losing membership.

Slovo on a Roll

Behind the vast success of the communists stands one man — Joseph Slovo. This Lithuanian and former KGB colonel who took over the leadership of the ANC in 1985, has now successfully drawn the National Party into an alliance with the South African Communist Party. It is only a matter of time before the alliance becomes one party — the South African Communist Party.

The way Slovo has remained behind the scenes while using Mandela and de Klerk to shield himself is undoubtedly brilliant. He is the mastermind *par excellence*. Behind the scenes, he presides over a 14-member Inner Communist Council made up of seven whites and seven Indians. These are the men and women who are behind the black-on-black violence. It is in their best interest to keep blacks fighting among themselves.

If a communist government comes to power in South Africa, this Inner Communist Council will run the country from behind the scenes. Black communists, including Mandela, will be mere surrogates, as they are now.

It is, however, no easy march for Slovo, to his cherished goal of transforming South Africa into a communist state. He faces many obstacles, but one of them towers above all others: Mangosuthu Buthelezi.

In 1992, Buthelezi realized that the Nationalist government had effectively surrendered to the communists. He then formed the Concerned South African Group (COSAG) — a group concerned about South Africa's descent into communism. COSAG is made up of Bophuthatswana, the Conservative Party, the *Afrikaner Volksunie*, Ciskei, and Inkatha Freedom Party. If South Africa is to be spared from communism, this is the group which will do it.

There is talk about South Africa having its first democratic elections in April 1994. Whether the elections will actually be held is doubtful. It is hard to see how campaigning will take place when private armies are running rampant throughout the country and violence is escalating.

If and when elections are held, South Africans will have a clear choice between the Nationalist Party/South African Communist Party Alliance and the Concerned South African Group representing democracy.

If South Africans want a bright future, they will have to accomplish three major tasks with their votes:

First, they will have to formally vote the National Party out of office. A party cannot change its essential character. National Party and apartheid are synonymous. Even if the victims have forgiven it, the party remains evil. It can never be otherwise.

Members of the party can and should change. They will demonstrate their change of heart by resigning from the

National Party and joining a party which holds promise and hope for a new future. Since the party failed to disband, it is left to the voters to put an end to a very dark chapter in South Africa's history.

Had South Africa been a democracy in 1948, the National Party would never have won the election with its apartheid platform and de Klerk would never have been President. At the earliest opportunity, the voters must drive that point home. It would be a travesty to have the National Party as part of any future South African government.

Second, the ANC communists have one objective which has nothing to do with power-sharing. They want complete and absolute power. Communism is infinitely worse than apartheid. I discovered this when I lived and studied in Czechoslovakia in the 1960s. The voters who want democracy have an obligation not to vote for the communists. Otherwise they will be cutting their own throats.

They only have to ponder what the communists have done in Mozambique and Angola. Then they must examine the record of the ANC communists since 1990. It is a record full of unspeakable atrocities.

Third, South Africans will need to vote for a party or a combination of parties which will offer them a new beginning. That new beginning should demonstrate a complete break with apartheid South Africa. The new South Africa will have to be a federal state built on the foundation of a multi-party democracy, fueled by capitalism, and protected by a bill of rights.

South Africans will have to ponder very seriously the catastrophic consequences of a government which combines two of the world's most evil systems — apartheid and communism. That is what the unholy alliance of de Klerk, Mandela, and Slovo represents.

The choices for South Africans are crystal clear: democracy or communism; freedom or slavery; life or death. That is what it all comes down to.

Conclusion

Three years have passed since F.W. de Klerk announced that apartheid was to be dismantled. The announcement was supposed to usher in a new era of political debate, discussion, accommodation, and cooperation among the various political parties. Negotiations which would give birth to a new peaceful South Africa would be conducted in a spirit of give and take. Differences would be buried; past sins forgiven, even if not forgotten; there would be a common purpose to lay a firm foundation for a democratic, nonracial, prosperous, and peaceful South Africa.

This was the hope of many South Africans. It was perhaps too optimistic, if not unrealistic. During the harsh years of apartheid, optimists often spoke about the deep "reservoir of goodwill" among South Africans of all races, especially black South Africans. We were unaware of the fact that in order to cope in what was virtually a police state, many black South Africans developed what almost became a natural mechanism to conceal their feelings. This is especially true of the older generation. They wore masks.

Underneath the masks, however, they were seething with anger and writhing in hatred. They wanted revenge. This is especially true of the younger generation. The ANC communists, in their bid for absolute power, will exploit this anger and hatred to the fullest. What de Klerk did on February 2, 1990 was effectively to remove the masks and open the lid which had prevented the anger and hatred from exploding. There are more blacks who want nothing else but revenge than the so-called political experts are prepared to admit.

Whites, on the other hand, are fearful that South Africa will become another ruined African state like Somalia or Liberia; fearful that they will lose all they have built — as happened in Algeria, the Belgian Congo, Angola, and Mozambique; fearful even that they will be driven into the sea. Others have simply become prisoners of guilt.

Wherever I go, people ask the same question: "What will happen in South Africa?" One does not have to be a prophet to know that the combination of fear and hatred spells disaster.

In the short term, the prospects for South Africa are bleak. There is not going to be anything approaching a smooth transition from apartheid to democracy. Violence will play a major role in determining the future. There is already a low intensity civil war taking place in the country, and the government of F.W. de Klerk is a government in name only.

A government which can not protect its citizens is worthless and illegitimate. The ongoing violence will lead to one of several outcomes. If the number of whites killed increases dramatically, there will be some form of military takeover. It will either be the South African Defense Force, white private armies, or both. Such a step would lead to the suspension of whatever constitution the country might still have and martial law will be declared.

Contrary to what many commentators believe, such a step would not lead to a full-scale civil war. In fact, if the the military is able to reestablish discipline in the country, the takeover would be welcomed by large sections of the South African population. A full-scale civil war is a possibility if the fighting between supporters of the ANC and Inkatha does not end. A civil war in South Africa will pit black against black as happened in Ethiopia, Somalia, Uganda, Liberia, Mozambique, Rwanda, Zaire, and Angola.

CONCLUSION

If the negotiations which have been going on for almost two years are any measure, the elections will be a farce. They will be rigged to produce an outcome predetermined by the de Klerk government, and the so-called international community. This also could lead to civil war. Contrary to popular thought, this would not be a war between whites and blacks. There would be whites and blacks on each side, and it would be Africa's most destructive war.

There are no quick answers to South Africa's problems, no easy solutions. The choice South Africans have is clear: Find workable solutions peacefully or plunge the country into a bloody revolution. What is required is a complete change in attitude — a conversion. For the moment, at least, South African negotiators are laying the foundation for a revolution. The march to slavery has begun.

APPENDIX I

"How to Be a Good Communist"

— by Nelson Mandela

Editor's Note: *Nelson Mandela is known throughout the world as a champion of democracy and freedom. Little, though, is known about his adherence and dedication to the communist philosophy. The words of this appendix belie the image which the international media has shaped and molded for Nelson Mandela. Keep in mind as you read: These are the very words of Mandela himself — uncensored and original.*

A Communist is a member of the Communist Party who understands and accepts the theory and practice of Marxism-Leninism as explained by Marx, Engles, Lenin, and Stalin, and who subjects himself to the discipline of the Party.

The goal of Communism is a classless society based on the principle: from each according to his ability and to each according to his needs.

The aim is to change the present world into a Communist world where there will be no exploiters and exploited, no oppressor and oppressed, no rich and no poor. Communists fight for a world where there will be no unemployment, no poverty and starvation, disease and ignorance. In such a world there will be no capitalists, no imperialists, no fascists. There will be neither colonies nor wars.

In our own country, the struggles of the oppressed people are guided by the South African Communist Party and inspired by its policies. The aim of the S.A.C.P. is to defeat the Nationalist Government, to free the people of South Africa from the evils of racial discrimination and exploitation, and to build a classless or socialist society in which the land, the mines, the mills....

Under a Communist Party Government, South Africa will become a land of milk and honey. Political, economic, and social rights will cease to be enjoyed by Whites only. They will be shared equally by Whites and Non-Whites. There will be enough land and houses for all. There will be no unemployment, starvation, and disease. Workers will earn decent wages; transport will be cheap and education free. There will be no pass laws, no influx control, no Police raids for passes and poll tax. Africans, Europeans, Coloureds, and Indians will live in racial peace and perfect equality.

The victory of Socialism in the U.S.S.R., in the People's Republic of China, in Bulgaria, Czechoslovakia, Hungary, Poland, and Romania, where the living conditions of the people were in many respects similar and even worse than ours, proves that we too can achieve this important goal.

Communists everywhere fight to destroy capitalist society and to replace it with Socialism, where the masses of the common people, irrespective of race or colour, will live in complete equality, freedom, and happiness. They seek to revolutionise society and are thus called revolutionaries. Those who support capitalism with its class divisions and other evils and who oppose our just struggle to end oppression and exploitation are called counter-revolutionaries.

Comrade Liu Hao Schi, member of the Central Committee of the Communist Party of China, says:

> "We Communist Party members are the most advanced revolutionaries in modern history and are the contemporary fighting and driving force in changing society and the world. Revolutionaries exist because counter-revolutionaries still exist. Therefore, to conduct a ceaseless struggle against the counter-revolutionaries constitutes an essential condition for the existence and development of revolutionaries. If they fail to carry on such a struggle, they cannot be called revolutionaries and

still less can they advance and develop. It is in the course of this ... members change society, change the world and at the same time change themselves."

To succeed in conducting a ceaseless struggle against the counter-revolutionaries and to be able to play the vital role of being the most advanced revolutionary and driving force in changing society and the world, one must put all else aside and seriously and faithfully undertake self-cultivation.

The Process of Self-Cultivation

The process of self-cultivation involves two elements:
I. One's steeling in the practical struggle of the oppressed people, and
II. The cultivation of one's ideas.

I. One's Steeling in the Practical Struggle of the Oppressed People

To become the most advanced communist revolutionary, it is not enough to understand and accept the theory of Marxism-Leninism. In addition, one must take part in the practical struggles of the people against oppression and exploitation. A person who is isolated from the people's struggles, an arm-chair politician, however deep his knowledge of Marxist theory might be, is not a communist revolutionary.

It is only in the course of such practical struggles that one's advancement and development is stimulated, that one acquires the necessary experience to guide the masses of the people in their political battles and the art and skill of being a driving force in changing society and the world. It is precisely for this reason that S.A.C.P requires its members to participate fully and without reservations in such issues as the Anti-Pass Campaigns, the struggle against Bantu Authorities, against job reservation, the Group Areas Act, and in all other mass campaigns.

By consistently taking part in such struggles, Party members who may ... gain valuable knowledge and get hardened for the stern mass struggles that are part and parcel of the life of every Communist revolutionary.

II. The Cultivation of One's Ideas

Participation (in) practical mass struggles does (not) in itself enable a Party member to raise his revolutionary qualities, nor does it help him to understand the (aims) of the development of society and the laws of the revolution. Progress in one's revolutionary qualities and knowledge of the laws of social development and the laws of the revolution will be achieved by a thorough understanding of the meaning of Marxism. It is thus absolutely imperative for all Party members to have to make a serious study of Marxist philosophy and to master it completely. Only in this way will Party members become the most advanced revolutionaries. Only in this way will they advance and develop.

The aim of studying Marxist philosophy is to enable us to direct more effectively revolutionary mass.... To put it in a nutshell, Marxism....

Communist Party members must undertake self-cultivation whether they are new members in the Party or old ones, whether they are workers, peasants, businessmen, professional men, or intellectuals, and whether they are conducting difficult or easy revolutionary mass campaigns; in victory or defeat.

Finally, self-cultivation must be imaginative and practical, and must be used to eliminate from one's outlook and conduct unhealthy tendencies which local conditions may give rise to.

South Africa is a country where the Whites dominate politically, economically and socially and where Africans, Coloureds, and Indians are treated as inferiors. It is a country torn asunder by racial strife and where black and white chauvinists find fertile soil in which it thrives and where efforts and appeals for working-class solidarity very often fall on deaf ears.

This pamphlet compiled by the S.A.C.P. to mark the fortieth anniversary of the Communist Party of South Africa which preceded the S.A.C.P. and which was declared illegal in 1950, correctly points out that, in spite of all the formidable difficulties that face it, the C.P.S.A. had in its existence brought about profound changes in the thinking and political outlook of the oppressed people of South Africa. These achievements are being expanded and further developed by the S.A.C.P.; the worthy successor of the C.P.S.A. In spite of these advances, however, there is still the danger that the historical problems and prejudices produced by capitalist society in our country may infiltrate into our Party and influence the political outlook of our Party members.

In cultivating their outlook, our members must consciously strive to remove these particular weaknesses and shortcomings as well.

This is what we mean when we say Party members must undertake self-cultivation.

How to Become the Best Pupils of Marx, Engles, Lenin, and Stalin

At the beginning of these lectures, we defined a Communist as a member of the Communist Party who understands and accepts the theory and practice of Marxism-Leninism as explained by Marx, Engles, Lenin, and Stalin.

Any person may become a member of the Communist Party if he accepts the Programme and Constitution of the Party, pays Party membership fees, and undertakes tasks given to him in one of the Party's organisations. These are called the minimum qualifications that every Party member must possess, but every one of our members should not be content to be a member of minimum qualifications. He must strive to become a member of maximum qualifications. Every Party member should raise his revolutionary qualities in every respect to the same level as those of Marx, Engles, Lenin, and Stalin.

Some say that it is impossible to acquire the great qualities of revolutionary geniuses like Marx, Engles, Lenin, and Stalin and that it is impossible to raise one's own qualities to the same level as theirs. But as long as Party members work hard and earnestly, never allow themselves to be isolated for one single moment from the day to day struggle of the people, and make serious efforts to study Marxist literature, learn from the experiences of other comrades and the masses of the people, and constantly strive to steel and cultivate themselves, they will be perfectly able to raise their qualities to the same level as that of Marx, Engles, Lenin, and Stalin.

There are two ways of studying Marxism. One is to learn it by heart and be able to repeat mechanically the information learnt without being able to use this information for the purpose of solving problems. The second is to try to master the essence, spirit, and methods of Marxism. In this second category belong those comrades who read over and over again Marxist literature, who pay special attention to the concrete conditions existing in the country where they live and draw their own conclusions, their ... activities, their attitude towards other comrades and the masses of the people, and the whole of their lives are guided by the principles of Marxism-Leninism and aimed at one thing -- national liberation, the victory of the working class, the liberation of mankind, the success of Communism, and nothing else.

To reach this goal calls for a supreme effort and an iron will. It means complete dedication to the struggle for the removal of oppression and exploitation and for lifelong dedication to the study of Marxism.

The Aspects and Methods of Cultivation

Cultivation must be carried on in all aspects in the course of the long and strenuous struggle to free the working class and the masses of the people from capitalist exploitation. Cultivation is needed in studying Marxism and in applying it to answer questions and to solve practical problems, in sharpening one's class outlook and political thinking, in shaping one's moral character and behavior; in hard work and ability to withstand hardship, in preserving the Party and complete dedication to the cause of the Communist Revolution.

The life of a Communist revolutionary is no bed of roses. It consists of serious studies in Marxist literature, of hard work, and of constant participation in numerous and endless mass struggles. He has no time for worldly pleasures and his whole life is devoted to one thing, and one thing only, the destruction of capitalist society, the removal of all forms of exploitation, and the liberation of mankind. A Communist revolutionary always combines thought with practice. He studies for the sole purpose of putting into practice what he has learnt. He regards Marxism as ... action and takes part fully and without reservation in mass struggles directed by the Party or by other political organisations outside of the Party. In South Africa, a Communist Party member must take part in mass struggles initiated by the S.A.C.P., the Congress Movement or by other political bodies within the liberation movement.

Relation Between the Study of Marxist-Leninist Theory and the Ideological Cultivation of Party Members

It is commonly thought that one's intelligence, ability, and the study of Marxist textbooks are in themselves enough to enable one to master the theory and method of Marxism-Leninism. Nothing could be further from the truth. Dealing with this point, Liu Shao Chu says:

> "Marxism-Leninism is the science of the proletarian revolution. It can be thoroughly understood and mastered

only by those who fully take the proletarian standpoint and who adopt the ideals of the proletariat as their own. It is impossible for anyone to thoroughly understand and master the strenuous study if he lacks the firm standpoint and ... ideals of the proletariat. This is also an obvious truth. Therefore, in studying the theory and method of Marxism-Leninism today, it is necessary that our study proceeds simultaneously with our ideological cultivation and steeling because without the theory and method of Marxism-Leninism, we should have nothing to guide our thoughts and actions and our ideological cultivation would also be impossible. These two are closely related to each other, and are inseparable."

We do need Communist Party members who are highly intelligent and who have ability and who make it their business to have a thorough understanding of Marxist theory. But a working class revolution will be carried out successfully by those Party members who, in addition to the characteristics mentioned above, adopt without reservation, the standpoint and ideals of the working class.

Although they may be unable to recite quotations from Marxist textbooks, experience shows that Party members of working class origin have a keener interest and deeper understanding of Marxism-Leninism than those Party members of student origin provided it is explained to them in words they understand. In loyalty to the Party, in discipline, and in the handling of practical problems, they often prove more correct and more in conformity with the Principles of Marxism-Leninism than others.

This is so because Party members of working class origin have a firm and pure Communist standpoint and ideals, an objective attitude towards things, and in their minds they have no preconceived ideas whatsoever, and no worries about personal problems or about impure matters.

Party members who lack a firm working class outlook, who have the habits ... of other classes and who have personal interests and selfish ideas, are not true Communists. As a matter of fact they very often find that Marxist-Leninism principles will clash with their interests, and they invariably try to distort these principles to suit their own personal interests and prejudices.

Every Communist revolutionary must, therefore, firmly adopt the standpoint and ideology of the working class. Unless he does this, it is not possible for him to understand the universal truth of Marxism-Leninism.

The Cause of Communism is the Greatest and Most Arduous Cause in the History of Mankind

At the beginning of this section we found out that our aim is to change the present world into a Communist world where there will be no exploiters and exploited, no oppressor and oppressed, no rich and poor. We also make the point that the victory of Socialism in the U.S.S.R., in China, and other States in Asia and Eastern Europe proves that a Communist world is capable of attainment. Moreover, since the victory of Socialism in the U.S.S.R. in 1917, the Socialist Camp has grown to become a world force with a population of more that 1,000 million and occupying a third of the Globe.

But in spite of this victorious advance, the Communist movement still faces powerful enemies which must be completely crushed and wiped out from the face of the earth before a Communist world can be realised. Without a hard, bitter, and long struggle against capitalism and exploitation, there can be no Communist world.

The cause of Communism is the greatest cause in the history of Mankind, because it seeks to remove from society all forms of oppression and exploitation of mankind, and to ensure peace and prosperity to all.

A Communist revolution is different from all other revolutions in history. Whereas in other revolutions the seizure of State Power is an end in itself, in a Communist revolution the seizure of State Power by the working class is a means to an end, that end being the total removal of all forms of exploitation, the liberation of mankind by building up a classless society.

Every Communist Party member must possess the greatest courage and revolutionary determination and must be prepared to play his part and carry out all political activities ... without fear or hesitation.

In the struggle to transform the present world into a Communist world, we must strive consistently to combine theory with practice.

Finally, we must live and develop in reality. In fighting to change the world we must start from the very people in close contact with us. We must thoroughly study our own situation and problems, understand them completely, and work out appropriate solutions.

The Unconditional Subordination of the Personal Interests of a Party Member to the Interests of the Party

A Communist Party member must subordinate his personal interests to those of the Party. The Communist Party has no interests of its own apart from those of the working class. The Party seeks to destroy capitalist exploitation and to free the working class. Therefore, the subordination of a Party Member's personal interests to the Party's interests means subordination to the interests of the working class.

We test a Communist Party member's loyalty to the Party, to the revolution and the Communist cause by the manner in which he absolutely and unconditionally subordinates his interests to those of the Party under all circumstances. To sacrifice one's personal interests and even one's life without hesitation for the cause of the Party is the highest manifestation of Communist ethics.

In the Party our members should not have personal aims independent of the Party's interests. The desire for personal power and positions, individual heroism conflicts with the interests of the Party and the working class.

APPENDIX I

A true Communist should possess the following characteristics:

(1) He must possess very good Communist ethics.

He can show love and loyalty to all his Comrades, revolutionaries, and working people, help them unconditionally, treat them with equality, and never harm any one of them.

He always tries to do more revolutionary work than others and to fight harder. In times of adversity he will stand out courageously and unflinchingly and, in the face of difficulties he will demonstrate the greatest sense of responsibility. He is able to resist corruption by riches or honours, to resist tendencies to vacillate in spite of poverty and lowly status, and to refuse to yield in spite of threats of force.

(2) He possess (sic) the greatest courage. He can see his mistakes and shortcomings and has sufficient willpower to correct them. At all times and under all circumstances he speaks the truth and nothing but truth. He courageously fights for it even when it is temporarily to his disadvantage to do so.

(3) He has a thorough understanding of the theory and method of Marxism-Leninism. He has an objective attitude.

(4) He is the most sincere, most candid, and happiest of men. Apart from the interests of the Party and of the revolution he has no personal losses or gains or other things to worry about. He takes care not to do wrong things when he works independently and without supervision and when there is ample opportunity for him to do all kinds of wrong things.

He does not fear criticism from others and he can courageously and sincerely criticise others.

(5) He possesses the highest self-respect and self-esteem. For the interest of the party and of the revolution, he can also be the most lenient, most tolerant, and most ready to compromise and he will even endure, if necessary, various forms of humiliation and injustice without feeling hurt or bearing grudges.

The Communist Party represents not only the interests of individual Party members but also the long-range interests of the entire body of workers and the emancipation of mankind; the Communist Party has no other interests and aims. The Party must not be regarded as a narrow small group like a guild which seeks only the personal interests of its members. Whoever holds such a view is not a Communist.

A member of our Party is no longer just an ordinary person. He is a conscious vanguard fighter of the working class. He should prove himself a conscious living representative of the interests and ideology of the working class. He should thoroughly merge his personal interests and aims in the general interests and aims of the Party and the working class.

A Communist revolutionary has his personal interests and the Party should neither eliminate his personality nor prevent personal development, as long as these do not conflict with the interests of the Party.

This is what is meant by the unconditional subordination of the personal interests of a Party member to the interests of the Party.

Examples and Origin of the Various Kinds of Erroneous Ideologies in the Party

People who join the Communist Party come from different classes of society and bring with them various habits and prejudices which often clash with the basic tenets of Marxism-Leninism. Because these people do not have a firm and clear-cut Communist outlook they very often waiver and even desert the Party when they are faced with danger or difficulties.

The Party must pay particular attention to the education, steeling, and self-cultivation of such comrades since without them, they cannot develop to be true Communists. No Communist Party anywhere in the world limits its membership only to those who have a thorough understanding of Communism. The Party will admit any person who accepts the programme of the Party and its Constitution. By serious study and hard work such comrades can develop into excellent

Communists ready to give their lives for the Party and the Communist cause....

Individualism frequently expresses itself in unprincipled discussions and disputes, factional struggles, and in sectarian tendencies and in undermining Party discipline. A closely related mistake is that of departmentalism, in which comrades see only partial interests, sees only his part of the work instead of seeing the situation as a whole and of the work of others. It often leads to obstruction and must be avoided.

Others show conceit, individual heroism, and like to show off. Liu Shao Chu says of these people:

> "The first consideration of people with such ideas is their position in the Party. They like to show off, and want others to flatter them and admire them. They have personal ambition to become leaders. They take advantage of their abilities and like to claim credit; to show off themselves; to keep everything in their hand and they are intolerant. They are full of vanity, do not want to keep their heads in hard work and are unwilling to do technical work. They are haughty. When they have made some small achievements they become very arrogant and domineering as if there were no one else like them in the world. They seek to overshadow others and cannot treat others on equal terms, modestly and politely. They are self-conceited and like to lecture others, to instruct and boss others. They are always trying to climb above others, and do not accept directions from others, do not learn modestly from others and ... from the masses nor do they accept criticism from others. They like to be "promoted" but cannot stand being "demoted." They can only work in fair weather but not in foul. They cannot bear attacks on injustices and are unable to adapt themselves to circumstances. They are not great men capable of asserting themselves when necessary or of keeping in the background when required."

A Communist should have none of these shortcomings. Whoever possesses such weaknesses does not understand Communism and cannot rise to become as great as Lenin. In the Communist Party leaders achieve success through mass support. Mass support is earned by those Party members who have no personal interests as against those of the working class and the Party who are completely loyal to the Party, who have a high degree of Communist ethics and revolutionary qualities, who strive to master the theory and methods of Marxism-Leninism, who have considerable practical ability, who can actually direct Party work, who are not afraid of serious study, and love work, and who become heroes and leaders in the Communist revolution because of the confidence and support they enjoy from the masses of the people.

The struggle to change the ... world into a Communist world cannot be carried out by one person however able he may be and however hard he works. It can be carried out successfully only by the planned and combined efforts of millions of people.

Some Party members are contemptuous of technical work within the Party. Such an attitude is incorrect because technical work forms an important part of Party work and because a Party member should be ready and willing to do any work which is important to the Party whether or not he likes such work.

Other comrades within the Party reflect the ideology of the exploiting classes in their Party work, and in their relations with other Party members they behave like landlords, capitalists, imperialists, and fascists.

These persons seek to develop themselves by holding down others. They are jealous of those who are more capable. They are not prepared to work under other comrades or to take instructions. They secretly rejoice when other comrades fail in their political tasks and in their moral standards and conduct. They indulge in gossip and spread false information about their comrades. the Party. They should be fought and exposed wherever they are found.

The working class is entirely different from the exploiting class. It does not exploit others nor do its interests conflict with those of the Party and other workers of exploited masses.

The outlook and thinking of the working class are altogether different from those of the exploiting classes. In dealing with the enemies of the people they are merciless and uncompromising, but in dealing with their comrades they are always inspired by love and the desire to assist. They are strict with themselves but lenient towards other comrades. They are strict and firm on matters of principle and always adopt a frank and serious attitude. This is the outlook of the working class and should be learnt and developed by every Party member.

Some comrades still have bureaucratic tendencies. They like to run the Party by issuing edicts and directives without ... taking into account the views of other comrades. Such weaknesses are un-Marxist and every Communist should strive to overcome them completely.

Furthermore a Party member should be broad-minded and concern himself always with the overall situation when dealing with problems. He should avoid pettiness and unprincipled discussion. He should have ... standpoint and not be a fence sitter.

Although the Communist Party is the most progressive of all political parties, and although it fights for a society which guarantees happiness and prosperity to millions of people, not everything in it is perfect.... Its members come from the various classes of that society and some of them bring into the Party the habits, prejudices, and outlook on life of the class from which they came. It is precisely for this reason that Communist Party members must undertake self-cultivation. In addition to waging struggles against counter-revolutionary forces, the Party must carry on inner-Party struggle against those comrades who are still influenced by the outlook and prejudices of the exploiting classes.

The working class is commonly referred to as the proletariat. The working class can be divided into the three groups:

(1) The first group is composed of those who completely severed their ties with the capitalist class years ago. This is the core of the working class and are the most loyal and reliable.

(2) The second group consists of those who only recently came from the non-working class.... They are usually anarchistic and ultra-left.

(3) The third group is composed of the working class aristocracy, those working class members who are best provided for, who earn high wages, and whose economic position is comparatively high. They compromise easily with the enemies of the people, with the capitalist class.

Every Party member should aim to be the most loyal and reliable to the cause of Communism and to have a firm and clear-cut working class outlook.

The Attitude Towards Various Erroneous Ideologies in the Party and Inner Party Struggle

Some Party members have a pessimistic view on things and they see errors, defects, and a future beset with formidable difficulties and dangers. The growing strength of the Socialist Camp, the powerful influence exerted by our Party in our own country and the certainty of the final victory of Communism over Capitalism inspire them with no hope in the future.

Others see only victory and progress, and fail altogether to notice defects and errors in the Party. They become dizzy with success, become blindly optimistic and become less vigilant.

Both views are wrong and un-Marxist. A Communist Party member knows that the Communist Party is the most progressive and most revolutionary Party in the world. He has complete confidence in the future and he dedicates his entire career to the cause of Communism. In spite of this knowledge he realises most clearly that in our Party there are still various kinds of errors, defects, and undesirable things. A Party member clearly understands the origin of these errors and the method to be used in removing them.

The following are the various kinds of attitudes towards undesirable things in the Party:

(1) To enjoy seeing errors and defects in the Party and to magnify them to undermine the Party. This is the attitude of spies and similar elements within the Party.

(2) Some people consider that the existence of errors and defects in the Party is to their advantage and they deliberately help to spread them and to make use of them. This is the attitude adopted by opportunists and similar elements within the Party.

(3) To leave these errors and defects undisturbed instead of fighting against them. This is the course followed by those members who have but a weak sense of duty towards the Party and who have bureaucratic tendencies.

(4) To harbour violent hatred towards errors and defects and towards Party members whose political outlook is incorrect. They believe in bitter struggles among Party members and expel their comrades at the slightest pretext. This is the method used by Party comrades who do not correctly understand the methods of correcting mistakes and weakness amongst comrades.

All these attitudes are incorrect and dangerous and should be scrupulously avoided by Communists. Our own attitude is as follows:

(1) We first analyse the situation most thoroughly and decide which views are correct and which of them are incorrect and dangerous to the Party. Once we are convinced of the correct opinion we firmly uphold it to the bitter end and no matter how strong the opposition and how influential the individuals who hold the opposite point of view.

(2) Having carefully analysed the situation and having decided which is the correct opinion, we then devote our

attention to the promotion and development of the correct viewpoint. We never allow ourselves to be influenced by an incorrect point of view.

(3) Communists are men of action. In promoting and developing the correct viewpoint we also fight actively against all the undesirable things in life. A Party member who is afraid of action and hard struggle, however brilliant he might be, can never be a Communist revolutionary. A Communist must always and under all circumstances, be ready and willing to conduct an active struggle against all forms of reaction.

(4) Although a Communist never compromises on questions of principle, he never adopts an inflexible and mechanical attitude in his methods of struggle. The aim is always to reform and educate those comrades who still possess non-Communist tendencies.

(5) The elimination of undesirable tendencies in the Party and the building up of revolutionary qualities in our members enhances the discipline and prestige of the Party. Those Party members who fail to respond to the most patient persuasion and to efforts to educate and reform them, should be expelled from the Party.

As indicated at the very beginning of this series, a Communist is a member of the Communist Party who understands and accepts the theory and practice of Marxism-Leninism as expounded by Marx, Engles, Lenin, and Stalin, and who subjects himself to the discipline of the Party. A good Communist is therefore one who:

(1) Is a member of the Communist Party who is absolutely faithful and loyal to the Party, who obeys without question all Party rules and regulations, and who carries out all instructions issued by the Party.

(2) Has thoroughly studied the works of Marx, Engles, Lenin, and Stalin, who understands them clearly, and who knows how to carry out their teachings in the struggles of the people to defeat capitalism and all forms of exploitation.

APPENDIX I

(3) Devotes all his time to one thing, and one thing only, the struggle against Capitalism and for a Communist world.

(4) In their relations with Party comrades are always inspired by love and sincere friendship and the desire to be helpful.

(5) Are honest and upright and who are prepared to defend the truth at all times and under all circumstances.

Such is a good Communist.

APPENDIX II

The Communist Inner Circle

There are fourteen white and Indian members of the Communist Inner Circle. Seven are white and seven are Indian. The Circle is similar to the defunct Soviet Politburo. This is the most powerful group within the South African Communist Alliance and would actually run the country if the ANC were to come to power.

White

JOSEPH SLOVO: He is the brain behind the entire communist establishment and wields controlling power within the communist movement. He must be credited for taking over both the ANC and the National Party. He is a Lithuanian and a former Colonel in the KGB. He is personally responsible for the "armed struggle" and the ongoing slaughter of black opponents of communism. He headed MBOKODO and was responsible for the murder of young black South Africans in the ANC concentration camps.

RONNIE KASRILS "RED RONNIE": A committed terrorist and communist. His name is linked to terrorist attacks in South Africa as far back as the early 1960s. He is the one who led black youngsters into Bisho, Ciskei on a futile mission to overthrow the Ciskei government. Twenty-eight youngsters who were used as cannon fodder died in that reckless attempt and more than two hundred were injured.

JEREMY CROWN: A leading communist intellectual.

ALBIE SACHS: An intellectual and constitutional lawyer.

GILLIAN MARCUS: Spokeswoman for the communist establishment.

MARION SPARG: She was the first white South African woman jailed for terrorism. She is responsible for a series of bombings.

RAYMOND SUTTNER: Law professor.

Indian

SATHYANDRANATH (MAC) MAHARAJ: He is ranked as the most evil person in South Africa. Together with Joseph Slovo and Ronnie Kasrils, he was responsible for the atrocities in ANC death camps. He is also said to be the mastermind behind the black-on-black violence in South Africa. He hates Inkatha Freedom Party and the Zulus in particular.

AZIZ PAHAD: A graduate of the Lenin School in Moscow. At one time he headed the political-military committee of the communist party.

EBRAHIM ISMAIL EBRAHIM: A convicted terrorist.

BILLY NAIR: A leading convicted terrorist. Unrepentant.

AHMED KATHRADA: An original member of Umkhonto WeSizwe's high command.

DULLAH OMAR: A lawyer.

MOHAMED VALLI MOOSA: Communist Party's spokesman.

APPENDIX III

A Memorial of War

The following is a list of Inkatha Freedom Party Officials who were murdered between 1985 and June 1993. They are victims of a reign of terror unleashed by the ANC communists and condoned by the National Party government.

1. Mrs. Jane Mkhwanazi
Deputy-Treasurer
(Soweto/Zola North)
stabbed 1985

2. Miss N. Gumede
Secretary
(Dambuza) hacked
24/03/85

3. Mr. Chrophet Buthelezi
Vice-Chairperson
(Hare Wood) stabbed
21/04/85

4. Mr. S. Ndlovu
Chairperson
(Dambuza) stabbed
11/05/86

5. Mr. M. Ngoobo
Chairperson
(Sobantu) shot 1986

6. Mr. Msizi S'khosana
Vice-Chairperson
(PMB/Imbali Ward 4)
stabbed 13/06/86

7. Mrs. Evelyn Sabelo
WB Organiser
(Umlazi) shot 00/08/86

8. Mr. FT Dlamini
Central Committee
(KwaMashu) shot
28/10/86

9. Mr. Phineas Lembede
Deputy-Treasurer
(Sewula) stabbed 00/00/87

10. Mrs. Dinah Ndlovu
Treasurer (Mbabane)
(Munywini) stabbed
00/00/87

11. Mr. Mtolo
Publicity Secretary
(Inanda Newtown) stabbed
00/00/87

12. Miss Bongiwe Ndaba
Committee member
(Willowfontein) stabbed
00/00/87

13. Mr. Thulani Majola
YB Committee*
stabbed 1987

14. Mr. Eliot Mnowabe
YB Committee
(Dambuza) stoned/stabbed
1987

15. Mr. Shadrack Dlamini
Chairperson
(KwaMakutha) petrol
bombed 01/01/87

16. Mr. N. Ngubane
Treasurer
(Mpumalanga) shot
02/03/87

17. Mr. Nooleni Shange
Chairperson
(Woody Glen) stabbed
12/03/87

18. Mr. Sizwe Zondi
Organiser
(PMB/Imbali Stage 1) shot
05/05/87

19. Mr. Joseph Duma
Committee member
(PMB/Sweetwaters) shot
05/05/87

YB - Youth Brigade

20. Mr. Bhekithemba
Nene
Organiser
(KwaMncane) hit and run
05/06/87

21. Mr. S'busiso W Hill
YB National Executive
(Sewula) stabbed 28/07/87

22. Mr. OR Dlamini
Chairperson
(Inanda Newton) shot
07/08/87

23. Mr. Absolom Dlamini
Organiser
(PMB/Henley) stabbed
16/08/87

24. Mr. Khubeka
Chairperson
(PMB/Henley) stabbed
16/08/87

25. Mr. S Ngubane
YB Chairperson
(PMB/Sweetwaters)
stabbed 13/09/87

26. Mrs. Mlambo
Chairperson
(Emachobeni) stabbed
00/11/87

APPENDIX III

27. Mr. Nzuza
Chairperson
(Ekuthuleni) shot/stabbed
1988

28. Mr. Jan Ngoobo
Vice-Chairperson
(PMB/Mbabane) stabbed
00/01/88

29. Mr. M. Nkosi
Committee member
(Mpumalanga Ward 10)
necklaced 11/01/88

30. Mr. SS Cele
Chairperson
(Mpumalanga Unit 9)
burned 10/01/88

31. Mr. Mthethwa
Chairperson
(Mpumalanga Unit 4)
09/01/88

32. Mr. Moses Makhonya
YB Organiser
(Ntshongweni) stabbed
10/04/88

33. Mr. A. Mtolo
Chairperson
(Mpumalanga Ward 8)
hacked 10/05/88

34. Mr. Kumisani Awetha
Chairperson
(PMB/Imbali Ward 4)
16/05/88

35. Mr. "Five Cent"
Ndebele
Chairperson
(Inanda Newtown Ward 8)
necklaced 16/05/88

36. Mr. S'khwele Ngoobo
Deputy-Treasurer
(Munywini) petrol
bombed 23/05/88

37. Mr. Musa Mdlovu
YB Chairperson
(KwaPata) stabbed
00/07/88

38. Mr. B Dlamini
Chairperson
(Mpumalanga Unit 7)
necklaced 00/08/88

39. Mr. Hula Bhengu
Induna/Organiser
(Dindi) stabbed 06/08/88

40. Mr. Velenkosini
Mnomiya
Executive Committee
(Indanda Newtown)
decapitated 00/09/88

41. Mr. Nxumalo
Secretary
(Indanda Newton)
strangled 10/09/88

42. Mr. D.M. Mbanjwa
Chairperson
(KwaMakutha) shot
16/09/88

43. Mr. Mbele
Committee member
(Bhambayi) stabbed
20/10/88

44. Mr. S. Zikhali
Chairperson
(Tongaat) petrol bombed
30/12/88

45. Miss Thandeka Nkehli
YB Secretary
(Mpumalanga) shot
19/12/88

46. Mr. Mandla Zondi
Chairperson
(PMB/Slangspruit)
stabbed/shot 29/12/88

47. Mr. Danti Bhengu
Chairperson
(KwaNgoolosi) shot 1989

48. Mr. Phungula
Publicity Secretary
(Indanda) stabbed
00/00/89

49. Mr. M Mkhize
Organiser
(KwaNgoolosi) shot
00/00/89

50. Mr. B Mkhize
Publicity Secretary
(KwaNgoolosi) shot
00/00/89

51. Mr. Gwala
Vice-Chairperson
(Ezimangweni) shot/burnt
00/00/89

52. Mr. James Luthuli
Organiser
(Mpumuza) burned
00/00/89

53. Mr. Ntombela
Chairperson
(Umlazi) shot 00/01/89

54. Mr. Dladla
Vice-Chairperson
(Eduphakameni)
shot/burned 00/01/89

55. Mr. J. Majola
Secretary
(Ecabazini) shot/stabbed
04/01/89

56. Mr. Ntimbane
Vice-Chairperson
(Dalmeny Farm) 06/01/89

57. Mr. Luthuli
Vice-Chairperson
(Dalmeny Farm) stabbed
20/01/89

58. Mr. Khuzwayo
Publicity Secretary
(Dalmeny Farm) stabbed
07/01/89

59. Mr. Dlamini
Publicity Secretary
(Bhambayi) necklaced
10/01/89

60. Mr. M. Zondo
Induna/Organiser
(Inanda) stabbed 01/01/89

61. Mr. Sandile Sibiya
Secretary
(KwaMashu Ward 2)
shot/stabbed 02/01/89

62. Mr. Z. Mkhize
YB Publicity Secretary
(Inanda Newtown B)
stabbed 00/02/89

63. Mr. Mbuso Khubeka
Treasurer
(Ntshongweni)
shot/stabbed 00/02/89

64. Mr. Shabalala
Dep.Publicity Secretary
(Inanda Newtown) hacked
00/03/89

65. Mr. M Nzama
Publicity Secretary
(Inanda Newton) stabbed
00/03/89

66. Mr. S'du Ndlovu
YB Chairperson
(Mpumalanga) hacked
00/03/89

67. Mr. Zakhele Nkehli
Central Committee
(Mpumalanga Ward 4)
shot 03/03/89

68. Mr. Muzochithwayo
Gwala
Organiser
(Ntshongweni)
shot/burned 06/03/89

69. Mr. Cele
Chairperson
(Emawoti) shot 13/04/89

70. Mr. T.M. Ngubane
Chairperson
(Mpumalanga Unit 7)
stabbed 04/06/89

71. Mr. Phillip Blose
Induna/Organiser
(KwaNdwalane)
hacked/burned 19/06/89

72. Mr. Hezekiel Nxumalo
Chairperson
(Umlazi) strangled
10/09/89

73. Mr. Shelby Gwala
YB Chairperson
(Emophela) shot 17/10/89

74. Mr. Simon Buthelezi
Chairperson
(Swayimane) shot/stabbed
29/10/89

75. Mr. Soto Makhathini
Induna/Organiser
(Swayimane) shot/stabbed
29/10/89

76. Mr. M. Goumisa
Organiser (Swayimane)
shot 29/10/89

77. Mrs. Phakathi
Secretary(Inanda
Newtown C) stabbed
00/11/89

78. Mr. Hlongwane
YB Chairperson
(Inanda Newtown C)
stabbed/burned 00/11/89

79. Mr. Mhlongo
Executive committee
(Matikwe) shot 00/11/89

80. Mr. Buthelezi
Committee member
(Inanda) shot 00/11/89

81. Mr. Agrippa Gasela
Vice-Chairperson
(PMB/Imbali Ward 6) shot
06/11/89

82. Mr. D Manyoni
YB Secretary
(PMB/Imbali Ward 5)
decapitated 17/11/89

83. Mr. J Mtolo
Treasurer
(PMB/Imbali Ward 4)
stabbed 28/11/89

55. Mr. J. Majola
Secretary
(Ecabazini) shot/stabbed
04/01/89

56. Mr. Ntimbane
Vice-Chairperson
(Dalmeny Farm) 06/01/89

57. Mr. Luthuli
Vice-Chairperson
(Dalmeny Farm) stabbed
20/01/89

58. Mr. Khuzwayo
Publicity Secretary
(Dalmeny Farm) stabbed
07/01/89

59. Mr. Dlamini
Publicity Secretary
(Bhambayi) necklaced
10/01/89

60. Mr. M. Zondo
Induna/Organiser
(Inanda) stabbed 01/01/89

61. Mr. Sandile Sibiya
Secretary
(KwaMashu Ward 2)
shot/stabbed 02/01/89

62. Mr. Z. Mkhize
YB Publicity Secretary
(Inanda Newtown B)
stabbed 00/02/89

63. Mr. Mbuso Khubeka
Treasurer
(Ntshongweni)
shot/stabbed 00/02/89

64. Mr. Shabalala
Dep.Publicity Secretary
(Inanda Newtown) hacked
00/03/89

65. Mr. M Nzama
Publicity Secretary
(Inanda Newton) stabbed
00/03/89

66. Mr. S'du Ndlovu
YB Chairperson
(Mpumalanga) hacked
00/03/89

67. Mr. Zakhele Nkehli
Central Committee
(Mpumalanga Ward 4)
shot 03/03/89

68. Mr. Muzochithwayo
Gwala
Organiser
(Ntshongweni)
shot/burned 06/03/89

69. Mr. Cele
Chairperson
(Emawoti) shot 13/04/89

70. Mr. T.M. Ngubane
Chairperson
(Mpumalanga Unit 7)
stabbed 04/06/89

71. Mr. Phillip Blose
Induna/Organiser
(KwaNdwalane)
hacked/burned 19/06/89

72. Mr. Hezekiel Nxumalo
Chairperson
(Umlazi) strangled
10/09/89

73. Mr. Shelby Gwala
YB Chairperson
(Emophela) shot 17/10/89

74. Mr. Simon Buthelezi
Chairperson
(Swayimane) shot/stabbed
29/10/89

75. Mr. Soto Makhathini
Induna/Organiser
(Swayimane) shot/stabbed
29/10/89

76. Mr. M. Goumisa
Organiser (Swayimane)
shot 29/10/89

77. Mrs. Phakathi
Secretary(Inanda
Newtown C) stabbed
00/11/89

78. Mr. Hlongwane
YB Chairperson
(Inanda Newtown C)
stabbed/burned 00/11/89

79. Mr. Mhlongo
Executive committee
(Matikwe) shot 00/11/89

80. Mr. Buthelezi
Committee member
(Inanda) shot 00/11/89

81. Mr. Agrippa Gasela
Vice-Chairperson
(PMB/Imbali Ward 6) shot
06/11/89

82. Mr. D Manyoni
YB Secretary
(PMB/Imbali Ward 5)
decapitated 17/11/89

83. Mr. J Mtolo
Treasurer
(PMB/Imbali Ward 4)
stabbed 28/11/89

84. Mr. Shame
Publicity Secretary
(Bhambayi) necklaced
20/12/89

85. Mr. M. Mbewu
Committee member
(Ezimangweni) necklaced
10/12/89

86. Mr. Nkosi
YB Committee member
(Ezimangweni) stabbed
03/12/89

87. Mrs. J. Hlophe
Deputy-Secretary
(Matikwe) burned
10/12/89

88. Miss Margaret Hlophe
YB Committee member
(Matikwe) hacked/burned
06/12/89

89. Mrs. Mbele
Treasurer
(Matikwe) burned
07/12/89

90. Mr. Babusi Gowensa
Induna/Organiser
(Mkhazini) shot 10/12/89

91. Mr. Green Gumede
Chairperson
(Matikwe) shot 00/12/89

92. Mr. Ben Khumalo
Vice-Chairperson
(Emawoti) stabbed/burned
00/12/89

93. Mrs. Khumalo
WB Vice-Chairperson
(Emawoti) burned
00/12/89

94. Mr. Mhlongo
Publicity Secretary
(Inanda Newtown B)
00/12/89

95. Mr. Mhlongo
YB Secretary
(Inanda Newtown B)
00/12/89

96. Mr. Ngiba
Executive Committee
(Ohlange) shot 00/12/89

97. Mr. Z Mkhwanazi
YB Secretary
(Ecabazini) shot 00/12/89

98. Mr. M Mthethwa
YB Publicity Secretary
(Ezimangweni) shot
00/12/89

99. Mr. L Mbonambi
Deputy-Secretary
(Ezimangweni) shot
30/12/89

100. Mr. Dlamini
Vice-Chairperson
(Ezimangweni) shot
04/12/89

101. Mr. Basi Msomi
Induna/Organiser
(Mkhanzini) shot 31/12/89

102. Mr. Moses Majola
Vice-Chairperson
(Ashdown)
(PMB/Sweetwaters) shot
1990

103. Mrs. D. Luthuli
Organiser
(Ndwedwe) burned 1990

104. Mr. W. Luthuli
Committee member
(Ndwedwe) burned 1990

105. Mr. Mbhele
Publicity Secretary
(Matikwe) burned 1990

106. Mr. Nzimande
Publicity Secretary
(Bhambayi) throat slit
1990

107. Mr. M Shinga
Chairperson
(Emawoti) shot 00/00/90

108. Mr. Z Phungula
Deputy-Secretary
stabbed 00/00/90

109. Mrs. D Dlamini
WB Committee member
(Ndwedwe) burned
00/00/90

110. Mr. T Nkwanyana
Publicity Secretary
(Ezimangweni) 00/01/90

111. Mr. Mzizi
Chairperson
(Inanda) throat slit
00/01/90

112. Mr. T Ngoobo
Vice-Chairperson
(PMB/Imbali Ward 3) shot
01/01/90

113. Mr. BP Mhlongo
Chairperson
(Umbumbulu) stabbed
11/01/90

114. Mr. Mgenge
Vice-Chairperson
(Bhambayi) 00/02/90

APPENDIX III

115. Mr. F. Mbongwa
Induna/Organiser
(PMB/Mbabane) shot
30/02/90

116. Mr. T. Ndlovu
YB Chairperson
(Ntuzuma) throat slit
01/02/90

117. Mr. B. Manyoni
Organiser
(PMB/Imbali) shot/stoned
07/02/90

118. Mr. L. Mhlongo
Publicity Secretary
(KwaMashu L) shot
09/02/90

119. Mr. H. Mzindle
Organiser
(KwaNdwalane) burned
10/03/90

120. Mr. J. Mbhele
Organiser
(KwaMdwalane) burned
10/03/90

121. Mr. Ngubo
Executive Committee
(Woody Glen)
stabbed/shot 30/03/90

122. Mr. M. Mooyi
Vice-Chairperson
(Emagabheni) shot
00/03/90

123. Mr. Dladla
Chairperson
(Ekuphakameni) stabbed
00/03/90

124. Mr. Msibi
Chairperson
(Ntuzuma) necklaced
27/03/90

125. Mr. Mlambo
Organiser
(Inanda 00/04/90

126. Mr. J Ndlovu
Organiser
(KwaNdwalane) burned
00/04/90

127. Mr. Sishonke
Ndwalane
Treasurer
(Ensimbini) necklaced
00/04/90

128. Mr. B Kati Ndlovu
Chairperson
(Siyanda) shot 00/04/90

129. Mr. Albin Ngoobo
Organiser
(Mthwalume) hacked
10/04/90

130. Mr. S. Ngoobo
Publicity Secretary
(Ndwedwe) shot 20/05/90

131. Mr. P. Ngoobo
Secretary
(Ndwedwe)
stabbed/burned 08/05/90

132. Mr. John Ntshangase
Chairperson
(Taylors Halt) shot
02/05/90

133. Mr. Drake Ntombela
Committee member
(Taylors Halt) shot
02/05/90

134. Mr. Mbukelwa
Mnowabe
Chairperson
(PMB/Imbali Stage 2) shot
16/05/90

135. Mr. Emmanuel
Mkhize
Chairperson
(KwaMashu) shot/stabbed
26/05/90

136. Mr. Gwala
Committee member
(Ndwedwe) stabbed
26/06/90

137. Mr. S'qhatha Nokwe
Chairperson
(Tongaat) stabbed
14/06/90

138. Rev. Timothy Xaba
Secretary
(Greytown) shot 09/06/90

139. Mr. S. Sibisi
Publicity Secretary
(PMB/Imbali Stage 2) shot
10/06/90

140. Mr. BB Mbhele
YB Secretary
(Emagabheni) shot
14/04/90

141. Mr. Khuzwayo
Organiser
(Umgababa) stabbed
17/06/90

142. Mr. AP Shange
Chairperson
(Azalia) throat slit
20/06/90

143. Miss B.
Secretary
(PMB/Imbali) shot
07/07/90

144. Miss P. Shandu
Secretary
(Umgababa) burned
20/07/90

145. Miss Z. Shandu
YB Committee member
(Umgababa) burned
20/07/90

146. Miss N. Shandu
Committee member
(Umgababa) burned
20/07/90

147. Mr. D. Mohunu
Secretary
(Umgababa) shot 04/08/90

148. Mr. S. Khumalo
Deputy-Secretary
(Ezimangweni) shot
24/08/90

149. Mr. M. Msani
Vice-Chairperson
(Emagabheni) shot/burned
20/09/90

150. Miss B. Majola
Secretary
(Greytown) shot 09/10/90

151. Mr. L. Lombo
Chairperson
(PMB/Mvundleni) shot
30/10/90

152. Mr. P. Mbatha
Chairperson
(Soweto/Dube) shot
10/11/90

153. Mr. C.C. Cele
Chairperson
(Meerbank) burned
14/11/90

154. Mr. K. Makhaye
Chairperson
(PMB/Sweetwaters) shot
01/12/90

155. Rev J.H. Ngoobo
Chairperson
(PMB/Smero) stabbed
1991

156. Mr. Jack Maphumulo
Chairperson
(Swayimane) shot 1991

157. Mr. Frank Dube
Organiser
(Mbubu) shot/hacked
10/02/91

158. Mr. P.
Organiser
(Mnkangala) hacked
10/02/91

159. Mr. Alfred Duma
Organiser
(Zayeka) hacked 10/02/91

160. Mr. Dumisane
Msindane
Organiser
(Zayeka) hacked 10/02/91

161. Mr. O. Ndwalane
Organiser
(Mbothsa) 08/03/91

162. Mr. M. Maphumulo
Vice-Chairperson
(Maqongqo) shot 24/03/91

163. Mr. Mkhize
Organiser
(Richmond) shot 29/03/91

164. Mr. P. Mthembu
YB Chairperson
(Vosloorus) shot 07/04/91

165. Mr. K. Lamula
YB Chairperson
(Soweto/Merafe) hand
grenade 07/04/91

166. Mr. Thulani Mlambo
Chairperson
(Transvaal) shot/burned
07/04/91

167. Mr. Ntanzi
Organiser
(Richmond) stabbed
09/04/91

168. Mr. S.J. Hlela
Chairperson
(KwaMashu hostel) shot
14/04/91

169. Mr. Moses Khumalo
Vice-Chairperson
(KwaMashu hostel) shot
14/04/91

170. Mr. M. Khumalo
Chairperson
(Soweto/Meadowlands)
shot 19/04/91

171. Mr. Z. Ngubane
Induna/Organiser
(Mpande) shot 29/04/91

172. Mr. K Mthembu
Induna/Organiser
(Umgababa) bombed
30/04/91

APPENDIX III

173. Mr. M Gasa
YB Chairperson
(Emalangeni) shot
18/05/91

174. Mr. Ntama Mtolo
Organiser
(Richmond/Ndaleni)
stabbed 27/05/91

175. Mr. V.C. Zulu
Chairperson
(Malukazi) stabbed
28/06/91

176. Mr. M. Nsidane
YB Treasurer
(Richmond/Patheni) shot
07/07/91

177. Mr. P.S. Nzimande
Organiser
(Swayimane)
stabbed/stoned 27/07/91

178. Mr. John Nzuza
Chairperson
(KwaMashu) Shot
03/08/91

179. Mr. Jotham Mkhize
Treasurer
(Mafakatini) shot 08/08/91

180. Mr. Matanyi Zondi
Chairperson
(Wembezi) shot 14/08/91

181. Mr. D.J. Ndlovu
Organiser
(Ixopo) shot 16/08/91

182. Mr. Sibusiso Bhengu
Secretary
(Umkamaas) stabbed
26/08/91

183. Mr. Nxele
Organiser
(Table Mountain) shot
28/08/91

184. Mr. Ndodi Thusi
Organiser
(Richmond/Ndaleni) shot
30/08/91

185. Mr. Absolom Zulu
Organiser
(Mjika) hand grenade
04/09/91

186. Mr. Elphas
Ndwandwe
YB Chairperson
(Phola) shot 13/09/91

187. Mr. Wilfred Sabelo
Publicity Secretary
(Ngwelezane) shot
08/10/91

188. Mr. Sabatha Zwane
YB Vice-Chairperson
(Wesselton) shot 09/10/91

189. Mr. Petros Ngoobo
Secretary
(PMB/Imbali) shot
12/10/91

190. Mr. Bangukufa Cele
Chairperson
(Mtengwane) shot
16/10/91

191. Mrs. Kedibone
Mokalao
Organiser
(Reagile) stabbed/burned
23/10/91

192. Mr. Nfunzelwa
Ngoongo
Organiser
(Umbumbulu) shot
03/11/91

193. Mr. Walter Ndlovu
Organiser
(Elandskop) stabbed
03/11/91

194. Mr. Mbhekiseni
Gwala
YB National Executive
(Secunda/Mbalenhle) shot
04/11/91

195. Mrs. Doris T Caluza
WB Secretary
(Matimatolo) shot
23/11/91

196. Mr. Mgoduso
Organiser
(Mathulini) shot 24/11/91

197. Mr. Wiseman
Mthembu
Organiser
(Mthengwane) shot
10/12/91

198. Mr. Canwell Ngidi
Chairperson
(Soweto/Dube) shot
16/12/91

199. Mr. Thomas
Goabashe
Chairperson
(Maqongqo) shot 17/12/91

200. Mr. Ndwalane
Monomo
Chairperson
(Murchison) stoned/shot
22/12/91

201. Mr. Mlozane
Mhlongo
YB Chairperson
(Empangeni) shot
02/01/92

APPENDIX III

202. Mr. Joshua Jezangeni
Chairperson
(Empangeni/Enseleni) shot
21/01/92

203. Mr. Winnington
Sabelo
Central Committee
(Umlazi) shot 07/02/92

204. Mr. Mandlala
Organiser
(KwaMbonambi)
shot/mutilated 08/02/92

205. Mr. Mnandi Dladla
Organiser
(Wembezi) shot 22/02/92

206. Mr. Simon
Siphosenkosi
Ngubana(Umlazi)
shot/stabbed 07/03/92

207. Mr. Elton Gumede
Organiser
(Esihlonyaneni) shot
20/03/92

208. Mr. Christopher
Ngwenya
YB Organiser
(Wesselton) shot 12/04/92

209. Mr. Tobias Mdlalose
Chairperson
(Isitingini) shot 15/04/92

210. Mr. John Khanyile
Organiser
(Enkanyezini) shot
27/04/92

211. Mr. Alson Gogo
Chairperson
(Soweto/Dube) shot
11/05/92

212. Mr. Simon Nxumalo
Chairperson
(Alexandra) shot 15/05/92

213. Mr. Robert Zungu
Organiser
(Esikhawini) hand
grenade/hacked 23/05/92

214. Mr. Nyela Dlamini
Induna/Organiser
(Richmond/Patheni) shot
30/05/92

215. Mr. Masenti Dladla
Organiser
(Richmond/Patheni)
burned 12/06/92

216. Mr. Alson Mbambo
Organiser
(Esikhawini) shot
13/06/92

217. Mr. Khumalo
Chairperson
(Mandini/Nembe) shot
14/06/92

218. Mr. Meshack Xaba
Committee member
(Burntville) hacked
20/06/92

219. Mr. Jotham
Mjabhiseni Mkhwanazi
YB Organiser
(Empangeni/Enseleni) shot
22/06/92

220. Mr. Shiyabekhala
Kweyama
Organiser
(Umbumbulu) shot
23/06/92

221. Mr. Mdelwa Joseph
Shozi
Organiser
(Umbumbulu/Folweni)
shot 23/06/92

222. Mr. Isaac Mswane
Treasurer
(Wembezi) shot 25/06/92

223. Mr. Bhabhalaza
Dladla
Organiser
(Murchison) shot 26/06/92

224. Mr. Zephariah
Jabulani Nxumalo
Organiser
(Umlazi U Section) stoned
28/06/92

225. Mrs. D. Thusi
Organiser
(Nomganga) shot 28/06/92

226. Mr. Johannes Matula
Organiser
(Richmond/Gengeshe)
shot 28/06/92

227. Mr. Samson Majola
Organiser
(Murchison) shot 28/06/92

228. Mr. John Mlondo
Organiser
(Empangeni/Sigisi) shot
03/07/92

229. Mr. Mvimvezeli
Mohunu
Chairperson
(Nomganga) shot/burned
04/07/92

230. Mr. Simelane
Committee member
(Odondolo) shot 10/07/92

APPENDIX III

231. Mr. Dominic Mhlongo
Organiser
(Umbumbulu/Ehtoleni)
shot 14/06/92

232. Mr. Wellington Ngovese
Chairperson
(Umlazi/Glebesland) shot 16/07/92

233. Mr. Oupa Smith
Publicity Secretary
(Boipatong) necklaced 16/07/92

234. Mr. Khulekani Magubane
Organiser
(Empangeni/Matshana)
shot 02/08/92

235. Miss Zoleka Miya
YB Secretary
(Alexandra) shot 10/08/92

236. Mr. Fana Nzimande
Chairperson
(Richmond/Mkhobeni)
shot 23/08/92

237. Mrs. Ntombizizwe Nzimande
WB Chairperson
(Richmond/Mkhobeni)
shot 23/08/92

238. Mr. Mapu Sosibo
Organiser
(Richmond/Ndaleni) shot 28/08/92

239. Mr. Z. Zuma
Committee member
(Kwayavu) shot 13/09/92

240. Mr. Bheki Shelembe
Secretary
(Enkanyezini) shot 08/09/92

241. Mr. Lolo Shezi
Organiser
(Hopewell) shot 09/09/92

242. Mr. Sigaza Dlamini
Chairperson
(Table Mountain) shot 15/09/92

243. Mr. Bheka Phoswa
Organiser
(Richmond/Gengeshe)
shot/decapitated 26/09/92

244. Mr. Mbovani Nxele
Organiser
(Richmond/Gengeshe)
shot 26/09/92

245. Mr. Namakwakhe Jili
Organiser
(Richmond/Gengeshe)
shot 26/09/92

246. Mr. Gideon Sibiya
Chairperson
(Ningizimu) hand grenade
29/09/92

247. Mr. Mthembeni Xulu
Organiser
(Ningizimu) hand grenade
29/09/92

248. Mr. Soloman Mlondo
Chairperson
(Emabhuyeni) shot
08/10/92

249. Mr. Thandazani
Nhlangulela
Chairperson
(Bhidla) shot 11/10/92

250. Mr. Ndondiya Elias
Ngoobo
Organiser
(Umbumbulu) stabbed
12/10/92

251. Mrs. Mbhedlembedle
Victoria Ngoobo
Organiser
(Umbumbulu) stabbed
12/10/92

252. Mr. Bhekuyise
Shandu
Organiser
(Empangeni/Eniwe) shot
15/10/92

253. Mr. Jotham Xaba
YB Deputy-Secretary
(Alexandra) shot 16/10/92

254. Mr. Alson Khanyile
Organiser
(Odlameni) shot 18/10/92

255. Mr. Zachariah
Bhengu
Organiser
(Odlameni) shot 18/10/92

256. Mr. Nicholas
Nzimande
Organiser
(Umbumbulu) shot
29/10/92

257. Mr. Robert Masando
Committee member
(Ezakheni) stabbed/stoned
19/11/92

258. Mr. Peter Msibi
YB Committee
(Ezakheni C Section)
stabbed/stoned 02/11/92

259. Mr. Velias Ndlovu
YB Chairperson
(Hlathikulu) shot
07/11/92

260. Mr. Timothy Sithole
Organiser
(KwaMakutha) shot
15/11/92

261. Mr. Themba
Mdakane
Deputy Secretary
(Ezakheni C Section) shot
11/12/92

262. Mr. Khubeka
Committee member
(Ezakheni D Section)
necklaced 13/12/92

263. Mr. Nhlalayenza
Ngoobo
YB Chairperson
(PMB/Imbali) shot
04/12/92

264. Mr. Anthony Zulu
Chairperson
(Ezingolweni) shot
16/12/92

265. Mr. Enoch
Mkhwanazi
Organiser
(Empangeni) stabbed
23/12/92

266. Ms Bongekile Xulu
WB Chairperson
(Empangeni) shot
23/12/92

267. Mr. Msweli
Organiser
(KwaNzuza) shot
23/12/92

268. Mr. Madudu
Khumalo
Publicity Secretary
(Msitsheni) necklaced
12/01/93

269. Mrs. Sesi Khumalo
WB Organiser
(Tembisa) shot 06/01/93

270. Mr. France Mlaba
YB Chairperson
(Sundumbili) shot
12/01/93

271. Mr. Mthokozisi
Duma
YB Organiser
(Kwayuvu) shot 15/01/93

272. Mr. Silomo Gazu
Publicity Secretary
(Boipatong) necklaced
28/01/93

273. Mr. Andries Khoza
YB Regional Dep-Secr
(Tigane) shot 12/01/93

274. Mr. Khandalesizwe
Cele
Organiser
(Ezingolweni) decapitated
22/02/93

275. Mr. Mbongeleni Zulu
Committee member
(Muzawula) petrol bombed
28/02/93

276. Mr. Francis Bhekani
Mvelase
YB Committee
(Ezakheni) necklaced
01/03/93

277. Mr. John Thembani
Convenor
(Umlazi CC Section) shot
18/03/93

278. Mr. Roy Mpisane
Convenor
(Umlazi CC Section) shot
18/03/93

279. Mr. Alfred Miya
Chairperson
(Emashini) hand grenaded
23/03/93

280. Mr. Robert Sikobe
Branch Secretary
(Umlazi Unit 17) shot
23/03/93

281. Mr. Ephriam Ndebele
Organiser
(Umlazi) shot 23/03/93

282. Mr. Siphiwe Gumede
KLA member
(Ubombo) shot 04/04/93

283. Mr. Ciaphus Dlamini
Regional Chairperson
(KwaMbonambi) shot
16/04/93

284. Mr. Leonard Ngubo
Vice-Chairperson
(Ntuzuma) shot 21/04/93

285. Mr. M.J. Cele
Branch Secretary
(Umlazi Ward 2) shot
13/05/93

286. Mr. Jabulani Kunene
YB Vice-Chairperson
(Zonkizizwe) shot
21/05/93

APPENDIX III

287. Mrs. Julia Siphiwe
Mtshali
Branch Secretary
(Kwesine)
(Phola Park)
stabbed/necklaced
24/05/93

288. Mr. Zakhele Phineas
Luthuli
Vice-Chairperson
(Matshana) shot 27/05/93

289. Mr. Ishmael Bojosi
Organiser (Zone 7)
(Sebokeng) shot 28/05/93

290. Mr. Marcus
Makhanya
YB Chairperson
(Hopewell) shot/burned
29/05/93

291. Mr. Ndabazini
Nzama
Treasurer (Nobanga)
(Ndwedwe/KwaWosiyana)
shot 03/06/93

292. Mr. Paul Dintoe
YB Chairperson
(Ipelegeng) stabbed
05/06/93

293. Mr. Mkhombiseni
Buthelezi
Chairperson
(KwaMtetwa/Ekusayeni)
shot 06/06/93

294. Mr. Moupheni Zulu
Organiser (Emathulini)
(Ozwathini) shot 06/06/93

295. Alphaeus Buthelezi
Executive Committee
(Vosloorus) stabbed/shot
16/06/93

296. Mandla Mtshali
Committee Member
(Wembezi) shot
20/06/93

297. Petrus Roy Masinya
Branch Chairman
(Tembisa) shot
03/07/93

298. Patrick Khanyile
Branch Deputy Secretary
(Tembisa) shot
04/07/93

299. Bonginkosi Sithole
Chairperson (Tembisa)
shot 06/07/93

300. Mr. Japan Mzotho
Chairperson
(Gamalakhe/Qinabout)
shot 14/07/93

301. Tollman Khawula
Chairperson
(Paddock/Mqantsheni)
shot 10/07/93

302. Mavovo Mgobese
Chairperson (Ngema)
(Katlehong/Kwesine)
hacked 25/07/93

303. Absolom Shozi
Constituency Chair
(Katlehong) burned
25/07/93

304. Wilson Lombo
Deputy Treasurer
(Taylor's Halt)
shot 01/08/93

305. Mr. Sithelo Khumalo
YB Chairperson
(Osizweni) shot
03/08/93

306. Simon Mazibuko
Chairperson
(Tokhoza) shot
07/08/93

307. Simon Coba
Organizer
(Hlanganani/Amaqadi)
shot 09/08/93

308. Elias Dladla
Chairperson
(Ekusayeni) shot
07/09/93

309. Mr. Ethelbert
Malinga
Chairperson; shot
15/09/93

The carnage has not stopped. Despite the fact that Nelson Mandela has been awarded the Nobel Prize for Peace (1993), the supporters of his organization have now murdered over 300 Inkatha Freedom Party officials.

APPENDIX IV

The Freedom Alliance

On October 6, 1993, the parties of the COSAG group entered into a much more formal alliance. They transformed into the Freedom Alliance. The members include the Inkatha Freedom Party, the Conservative Party, The Afrikaner Volksfront, Bophuthatwsana, Ciskei, and other minor participants.

Before this, the various parties negotiated with the government and the ANC/SACP alliance bilaterally. With the formation of the Freedom Alliance, all began speaking through a single spokesman only.

The Freedom Alliance gives the peoples of South Africa great hope the NP/ANC/SACP juggernaut can be stopped and the descending communization of South Africa can be defeated.

Following are the solemn words of the Freedom Alliance Manifesto:

We, the parties and organisations of the Freedom Alliance, commit ourselves to work within our respective policies, ideologies and political visions and to achieve the goals set forth in this Manifesto so as to ensure long-lasting peace, freedom and democracy in Southern Africa.

We declare our commitment to the following principles:

a. The recognition of the guidance of Almighty God in the affairs of men and of nations;

b. The recognition of the right of self-determination of the peoples of Southern Africa;

c. The preservation of law, order and constitutionality;

d. Protection and promotion of free-market enterprise and private ownership and the commitment to eradicate poverty;

e. Rejection of (i) the notion of unitary state;
   (ii) racism, discrimination and sexism;
   (iii) any form of communism, totalitarianism and tyranny over the freedom of man and society;

And we therefore commit ourselves to the following goals;

1. Free and democratic elections in Southern Africa shall be held only under the parameters of final constitutions which;
   — entrench limits to power of government;
   — entrench checks and balances limiting the power of the state;
   — further individual and collective rights.

2. The political settlement reached in the final constitutional dispensation shall not be repealed or modified by a Constituent Assembly or a similar body.

3. Southern Africa shall be organised in member states which are primarily responsible for governance of the peoples to express their rights to self-determination.

4. The power of all governments shall be constitutionally limited to preserve the integrity and pre-eminence of civil

society. The constitutional autonomy of social and cultural formations and other institutions of civil society shall be recognised and protected.

5. Constitutionalism and the rule of law shall prevail in Southern Africa. Moreover, rigid guarantees shall be entrenched to ensure the supremacy of constitutionalism and the rule of law.

6. Cultural diversity and the rights of people, both as individuals and as members of the social and cultural formations to which they belong, shall be nurtured and protected.

7. Boundaries of member states shall be determined by the peoples of such states and not by a centralised process of negotiations.

8. Constitutional problems of Southern Africa shall be resolved through negotiations based on consensus.

9. The use of referenda shall be confined to testing the acceptability to the people of constitutional proposals in respect of which consensus has already been reached on a multi-party basis.

10. Negotiations shall continue until a settlement is reached. No one shall cut negotiations short to accommodate their political objectives.

11. Any arrangements and mechanisms must conform to the parameters of the final negotiated constitutional settlement, and shall neither be finalised nor implemented until that final settlement is properly secured.

12. The rights of peoples (individual and collective), their fundamental needs and political aspirations shall not be compromised, but shall survive any arbitrary and unilateral attempts to disregard them. The peoples shall preserve their undeniable right of self-determination, which includes the right to challenge, in any internationally acceptable manner, attempts to thwart these inalienable rights.

Index

Africa for the Africans 7, 25
African dictators 50, 86
African National Congress (ANC) iv, v, 3-9, 12, 13, 16, 17, 19-57, 59-63, 65, 67-70, 72-74, 77-78, 84, 87, 89, 94, 97, 102, 104, 106-107, 111-112, 119-124, 126-134, 136-138, 140-141, 145-151, 154-159, 163, 165-167, 170-173, 178, 191-194, 196-198, 221, 222, 225, 248
African National Congress Youth League (ANCYL) 5, 22, 53
Afrikaans 5, 11, 34, 135
Afrikaner 2, 6, 19, 110, 112, 130, 133, 146, 195, 248
Afrikaner Volksfront 9, 248
Afrikaner Volksunie 112, 195
AIDS 91, 99, 100, 159, 172, 177
Anglican Church 12, 69, 72, 73, 123
Angola v, 32, 33, 35, 37-40, 42-44, 49, 74, 93, 112, 116, 122, 158, 165, 166, 192, 193, 196, 198
Anti-Apartheid Act 71, 95
anti-apartheid movement 31, 48, 83
apartheid iv, 3, 5, 6, 11-13, 16, 17, 23, 26, 30-34, 36, 37, 48, 51, 55, 56, 58, 71, 77-83, 86-90, 93-97, 101, 102, 103, 110, 111, 114-117, 119, 125, 126, 128, 129, 131, 140, 144, 145, 151, 154, 157, 164, 167, 172, 173-175, 177-181, 185, 186, 189, 190, 194, 195, 196-198
armed struggle 5, 28, 31-33, 37, 53, 55, 57-60, 62, 63, 69, 73, 127, 128, 130, 148, 149, 151, 167, 221
artificial boundaries 2
Azania People's Organization (AZAPO) 57, 146, 168
Azania People's Liberation Army (APLA) 7
beatings 40, 43
Biehl, Amy 7
Black Caucus 45, 71, 95, 96, 98, 103, 125
Black Consciousness Movement 37, 57, 165, 168

black nationalist 7
blacks 3-5, 7, 11-14, 20, 21, 24, 25, 29, 30, 56-58, 60, 61, 63, 68, 70-73, 80, 83, 86-89, 93, 97, 99, 104, 107, 110, 111-114, 116-119, 123, 125, 126, 128, 130, 134, 137, 140, 145, 157, 159, 160, 167, 169, 171, 172, 173-175, 179, 195, 198, 199
Boesak, Allan 67-69, 75, 114
Bophuthatswana 46, 56, 125, 156, 157, 195
Botswana 19, 33, 34, 37, 39-42, 44, 49, 89
British 2, 4, 19-21, 57, 90, 91, 110, 125, 126
burning 34, 59, 69, 74, 87, 128, 167, 168, 171
Buthelezi, Mangosuthu 5, 35, 55-57, 60, 61, 63, 73, 111, 112, 115, 123, 124, 125-137, 195, 225, 230, 245
camps 14, 34, 35, 37, 38, 43-46, 48-50, 112, 119, 156, 160, 165, 172, 191, 221, 222
Carter, Jimmy 85, 120
Castro 9, 64, 65, 121, 136
Central Intelligence Agency (CIA) 29
Chinese instructors 14
Christianity 12, 23, 27, 160
Warren Christopher 119
Ciskei 46, 56, 125, 145, 156, 157, 195, 221, 248
civil rights 90, 98, 99, 103, 105, 109, 114, 116-118, 125, 129
civil war 4, 6, 9, 28, 198, 199
Clinton Administration 45
cocaine 33, 67
CODESA iv, 143-149, 155-157, 159
colonialism 2, 19, 78, 82, 110, 178
coloreds 11, 24, 25, 29, 61, 157
communism 2, 9, 15-17, 23, 24, 53, 54, 59, 62, 63, 67, 68, 70, 89, 100, 119, 141, 172, 173, 185, 186, 189, 195, 196, 201, 206, 209, 212, 213, 216, 221, 249
Communist Party of South Africa (CPSA) 4, 8, 21, 23, 205
Congress of Democrats 24

INDEX

Congress of the People 24, 25
Conservative Party (CP) 5, 9, 112, 146, 150, 195, 248
Coretta 98, 105, 106, 114
corruption 32, 37, 68, 82, 91, 113, 159, 180, 181, 184, 186, 211
Concerned South African Group (COSAG) 1
culture 1, 22, 135, 143, 153, 168, 170
Czechoslovakia 14-16, 139, 173, 196, 202
De Klerk, F.W. 36, 46, 47, 51, 63, 81, 101, 129-131, 136, 140, 145, 146, 148, 149, 153, 155, 189-192, 194, 196, 197, 198, 199
defiance campaign 13, 24
democracy 6, 16, 23, 25, 35, 43, 51, 59, 64, 79, 81, 82, 84, 85, 88, 89, 115, 126, 132, 140, 141, 143, 144, 146, 147, 154, 156, 157, 159-161, 170, 180, 181, 190, 191, 195, 196, 198, 201, 248
Democratic Party 27, 112, 114, 130, 134, 136
Dhlomo, Oscar 134
David Dinkins 103
Dobruska 15
Dube 20, 102, 235, 238, 239
Durban 13, 52, 62, 72, 123, 132, 133, 143, 147
Dutch 2, 3
elections 3, 36, 111, 137, 139, 160, 193, 195, 199, 249
Episcopal Church 16, 118
European Community 192-194
firing squad 30, 39, 43
Freedom Alliance iv, 248
Freedom Charter 8, 24, 25, 147
Gandhi, Mahatma 4, 24
Germany 16, 33, 85, 193
Goldstone Commission 191
guerilla 48
Hani, Chris 40-42, 50, 64, 75, 145, 166
homelands 12, 56, 61, 125
Houston Post 120

human rights 32, 43, 45, 46, 48, 64, 85, 86, 120-122
Hussein, Saddam 9, 64, 65, 139
Indian 1, 6, 24, 28, 29, 77, 87, 88, 97, 126, 141, 145, 156, 157, 167, 168, 171-174, 221, 222
Inkatha Freedom Party (IFP) iv, 5, 6, 22, 46, 56, 57, 74, 104, 111-112, 123-126, 128, 129, 130-141, 147, 157, 168, 192, 195, 198, 222, 225, 247, 248
Inkatha Central Committee 133
Inkathagate 132, 134, 135, 137
integration 118
Jackson, Jesse 45, 97, 98, 101, 107, 114
Johannesburg 13, 14, 21, 23-25, 28, 29, 34, 36, 57, 62, 72, 132, 133, 134, 143, 147, 159, 170
Jordan, Paulo 50
Justice Mohamed 145
Kasrils, Ronnie 42, 221, 222
King, Dr. Martin Luther 98, 106
Kliptown 24, 147
Kotane, Moses 23
KwaZulu 125, 127, 131, 132, 156
Laka, Abeod M. 40
Laliso, Sipho Amos 40
Land Acts 20
Lawyers for Human Rights 45
Lesotho 19, 34, 89
liberals 7, 67-70, 107, 109-119, 122, 125, 137, 173
Lombo, Siphowe Bethuel 41
lost generation iv, v, 128, 160, 163, 164, 168, 172-174
Lutuli, Albert 13, 23-26, 28-30, 72
Maharaj, Mac 50
Mandela, Nelson iv, 13, 14, 22-24, 26-29, 35, 40, 47, 48, 51-65, 78, 89, 90, 97, 101, 103-106, 111, 114, 119-121, 124, 125, 127, 131, 136, 140, 145, 146, 148, 149, 155, 156, 159, 165, 167, 171-173, 194-196, 201, 247
Mandela Football Club 62

Mandela, Winnie 40, 105, 167
Mapu, Mandla 40
Marxism 22, 37, 138, 201, 203-209, 211, 212, 214, 218
Marxist theory 14, 15, 203, 208
Matanzima, Kaiser and George 56
Mbeki, Thabo 50
MBOKODO 33, 41-43, 45, 49, 148, 193, 221
Mda, Peter 22
media 2, 3, 7, 29, 31, 35, 43, 52, 57, 58, 68-70, 74, 75, 93, 103, 106, 107, 111, 124-126, 129-131, 133-135, 137, 140, 149, 171, 172, 201
Modise, Joe 33, 40, 50
Moroka 22
Moscow 8, 23, 222
Moshoeu, Gordon 36
Mozambique 32, 33, 35, 44, 49, 89, 93, 192, 196, 198
Naidoo, Jay 159
Namibia 33, 35, 89
National Executive Committee 23, 36, 50
National Party 4-7, 9, 23, 26, 36, 51, 111-113, 130, 140, 150, 151, 153, 154, 179, 184, 189-191, 194-196, 221, 225, 248
Ndebele 2, 227, 244
Nobel Prize for Peace 28, 47, 72, 74, 247
non-violence 27, 28, 127
Organization of African Unity 45
Pan Africanist Congress (PAC) 7-8, 13, 25-26, 30, 34, 37, 51, 56, 136, 146, 149, 168
Pango 37, 40
Patriotic Front 7, 8
Peace Accord 147, 149, 152, 153
Pedi 2
Qoi Qoi 2
Qoi San 2, 21
Quatro Prison 38, 40-44, 49, 122
race 51, 99, 107, 118, 174, 202

racism 8, 16, 43, 78, 79, 83, 84, 95, 99, 100, 104, 106, 114, 115-117, 140, 193, 249
Ramaphosa, Cyril 156
refugees 34, 42, 49, 70, 99, 177, 193

Rivonia 29
Robinson, Randall 71, 94, 103, 104, 114, 115, 125
Sanctions 5, 31, 57, 58, 60, 63, 69-73, 78-81, 83-90, 94-98, 100, 101, 114-117, 119, 128, 133, 136, 156
Seme 20, 126, 127
September, Reg 50
Shangaan 2
Sharpeville 13, 25, 77
Sisulu, Walter 22, 101
Skekana Alpheus Kheswa 42
Slovo, Joseph 30, 33, 35, 36, 50, 59, 123, 159, 194-196, 221, 222
Sotho 2, 11, 104
South African Communist Party (SACP) 4-5, 8, 9, 14, 17, 23, 26, 28, 29, 30, 35-36, 39, 46, 51, 57, 59, 60-61, 63, 64, 68, 74, 78, 101, 120, 123, 136, 145-148, 155-156, 158, 194, 195, 201, 248
South African Council of Churches 67, 68, 75
South African Defense Force 34, 198
South African Indian Congress 24
South African Native National Congress 4, 19
Soweto 62, 68, 71, 72, 80, 87, 159, 170, 173, 225, 235, 236, 238, 239
Spear of the Nation (MK) 4, 13, 14, 27-32, 53, 57, 63, 148, 155, 156
Sullivan, Rev. Leon 70
Swaziland 2, 34, 89
Sweden 5, 47, 49, 193
Tambo, Oliver 22, 26, 30, 33, 41, 60, 124
Tanzania v, 14, 30, 33-35, 39, 41-44, 49, 74, 79, 112, 157, 165, 166

INDEX

terrorism 63, 65, 68, 103, 121, 130, 132, 166, 222
terrorist 53, 59, 112, 120, 148, 193, 221, 222
The Weekly Mail 133, 134, 137
torture 13, 36, 39, 40, 42-45, 48, 49, 156, 171, 193
trade unions 31, 87
Transafrica 45, 94-96, 102-104, 114, 125
Transkei 55, 56, 125, 131, 145, 157, 159
tribalism 20
Tswana 2, 55, 125
Tutu, Archbishop Desmond 67, 69-75, 114, 124, 165, 166
United Nations 16, 32, 42, 45, 49, 72, 77, 166, 192
United States iii, 16, 39, 49, 63, 64, 67, 104, 114, 121, 136
Unlawful Organizations Bill 23
Venda 2, 55, 56, 68, 125, 156
Victor Verster Prison 60
violence 3, 17, 23, 26-29, 31, 47, 53, 55, 61-63, 68, 73, 74, 78, 79, 85-87, 99, 100, 105, 111, 116, 118, 120, 121, 127-131, 136, 138, 147-149, 151-153, 159, 160, 169, 171, 191-193, 195, 198, 222
Washington, Booker T. 20, 102
World Alliance of Reformed Churches 69
World Council of Churches 69, 71
Xhosa 2, 11, 20, 33, 38, 55, 56, 104, 124, 125, 130, 131, 145
Xuma 22
Zambia v, 16, 17, 19, 33, 35, 42, 44, 49, 74, 79, 97, 112, 128, 165-167
Zimbabwe 27, 32, 33, 35, 89, 158, 165, 179, 193
Zulu 2, 5, 11, 20, 22, 23, 33, 56, 57, 73, 110, 111, 115, 123, 124-126, 130, 132-134, 136, 137, 140, 192, 237, 243-245
Zulu, Alphaeus 23, 73, 115

Bibliography

Books

- *The Amazing Mr. Fischer*; G. Ludi and B. Grobbelar, Nasionale Boekhandel, Cape Town, 1966, p. 8.

- *Black Politics in South Africa Since 1912*: p. 7.

- *A History of Communism in South Africa*: Henry R. Pike. Christian Mission International, Pretoria, 1985. p. 388.

- *What A Marxist South Africa Would Mean To You.* Aida Parker, Johannesburg, 1992. pp. 29-31.

Magazines and Newspapers

- *Citizen* (a Johannesburg daily newspaper), "37 Reds elected to top ANC body," July 8, 1991.

- *Economist* (a monthly British magazine), "The struggle continues," November 2, 1991.

- *Facts on File*, (a news reference service), "Political Exiles Granted Amnesty," November 14, 1991.

- *Johannesburg Star*, "TPA considers writing off R-762 million debt," July 13, 1990.

- *New York Times*, "Inquiry by Mandela's Group Finds Abuses by Its Forces," August 24, 1993.

- *New York Times*, "Mandela's Group Says It Won't Punish Rights Abusers in Its Ranks." August 31, 1993.

- *Time*, "The Lost Generation," February 18, 1993, pp. 48-51.